Cochrane
Marigold Library System

NOV - - 2013

BEST LOVED
BABY NAMES

and their meanings

D0049752

For my grandbabies

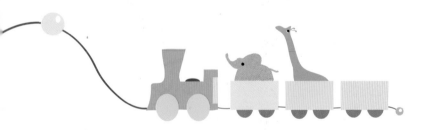

BEST LOVED BABY NAMES

and their meanings

Tracey Zabar

Illustrations by Claire Garland

spruce

Tracey Zabar designs charm bracelets for Barneys New York and Kate Spade, and provides jewelry for film, television, and theater. She lives in New York City with her husband and four sons. She is the author of *Charmed Bracelets*.

An Hachette UK Company
www.hachette.co.uk

First published in Great Britain in 2008 by
Spruce, a division of Octopus Publishing Group Ltd
Endeavour House, 189 Shaftesbury Avenue, London, WC2H 8JY
www.octopusbooks.co.uk
www.octopusbooksusa.com

This edition published in 2013

Copyright © Octopus Publishing Group Ltd 2005, 2008
Introductory text and name selection © Tracey Zabar 2005
Name entries (origins, derivations, and meanings) © Octopus Publishing Group Ltd 2005
Illustrations © Claire Garland 2005

Distributed in the US by
Hachette Book Group USA
237 Park Avenue
New York NY 10017 USA

Distributed in Canada by
Canadian Manda Group
165 Dufferin Street
Toronto, Ontario, Canada M6K 3H6

All rights reserved. No part of this work may be reproduced or utilized in any form or by any means, electronic or mechanical, including photocopying, recording or by any informa-tion storage and retrieval system, without the prior written permission of the publisher.

ISBN: 978-1-84601-449-9

A CIP catalogue record of this book is availlable from the British Library.

Printed and bound in China

2 4 6 8 10 9 7 5 3 1

NOTE TO READERS

This book features name selections compiled by Tracey Zabar. The author recognizes that names are continuously being invented, but this list is primarily a compilation of traditional names, with a sprinkling of new-age ones that sound perfect today.

Acknowledgments

Thanks to Sandy Gilbert Freidus, the most extraordinary editor and friend, and to Marc and Aaron for putting up with it all; to Claire Garland, for the most delicious illustrations; to Lara Comstock, who did research and corrections above and beyond my wildest expectations; to Zaro Weil, Ljiljana Baird, and everyone at MQ Publications in London and New York; to Hilary St. Clair Ney; Dervla Kelly, my expert on all things Irish; and Ellis Levine, the best literary lawyer ever there was.

To my cousin Larry Zilko, who retrieved thousands of words that my computer ate; to my nephew, Henry Zabar Mariscal, thank you for speaking Japanese; to Ronnie Butler, for inventing "Pay-Attention-to-Me-Day"; and Pequita. Oh, and Barneys and Kate Spade for selling all those bracelets so that I could have time to write.

To Karen Taffner Butler, Lisa Birnbach, Alexandra Trower Lindsey, and Brooke Garber Neidich, my buddies who think I'm more creative than I really am; to Cathy Darcy Hickson, Lee and Janice Princiotta, my childhood friends; and to the Colantropo and Carter families.

To the New York Public Library Irma and Paul Milstein Division of United States History, Local History, and Genealogy; the U.S. Social Security Administration, for keeping lists of the most popular names by decades; and to everyone who came through Ellis Island.

To my family: Nana, Bill, Taylor, Billy, and Max Blumenreich.

To the husband, David: thank you for letting me name those children anything I wanted; and to my hearts, Benjamin, Daniel, Michael, William, and Rebecca Maryrose. Let's have another baby! I know some great names . . .

Contents

Introduction

Best Loved Names

Here comes the baby! Things will never be the same. Life will be insane, exhausting, chaotic, and oh-so silly. You will spend hours pondering the mysteries of life: When will I ever get some sleep? How can something so little come with this much furniture? And toys. And footsie pajamas. And soooo many dirty…. Why aren't my friends endlessly interested in hearing how cute and fun this is? How did we ever live before, without our little angel? And, most importantly of all, what shall we name it?

Choosing a name for baby–this is a monumental decision. Do it right and it launches your little one into the world. Mess up, and there's a "kick-me" sign on little Ethlbert or Phnederera's forehead. Think about this! Children can be cruel. Even the kindest person can't resist a snicker when someone falls down. What's funnier than slipping on a banana peel? Well, that's what you're giving your child if you choose the wrong name. Do you want little Thorazine or Halitosis to come home crying every day? Of course not. So, get to work.

One Perfect Name

There are officially over a zillion names. If you eliminate all the names of bad politicians, greedy movie stars, misbehaving royals, the bullies in your third grade class, fun dog names, and all the great names that your sisters-in-law already stole (okay, used themselves), you are left with only about thirty. That's not bad, and, considering that your wee one is either a girl or a boy, that narrows it down to fifteen. Now, since you still have a little time, let's choose a name that you love . . . and that everybody else will be charmed by. Especially little Rebecca Jane or Joey. We need a sweet, tender name for the sweet, tender baby. Something unique, yet not weird. Timeless, classic, and not too trendy.

You know that voice in your head that tells you to eat chocolate, burgers, and potato chips all the time? Well, now it's telling you to find a delicious little name for your perfect little child. When you find it, you will whisper it to baby, and shout it out to the hills. It will be, well, perfect.

The Name Game

When you find that perfect name, do not, I repeat, do not tell anyone. I promise you that some mean relative will be reminded of the smelly boy in the fifth grade who picked his nose, and had the very same name. Or, your best friend will remember that nice girl from prep school who became a hooker. Or, the worst thing yet, your extremely evil cousin will name her child (or cat) the very same name, and claim she forgot you sent out those pre-birth announcements.

If someone does steal your name, don't get the voodoo doll out yet. I know, you named all your goldfish, your hamsters, and your dolls Christopher since you were four, and everyone knows that you would only consider Christopher or Christine for your first child. Then, five weeks before your due date, your sister-in-law names her baby Chris. What are you going to do? Just remember to buy drums for little Chris's first birthday, permanent markers and non-washable paints for his second birthday, a tank with spiders for the third . . . you get the picture.

And, there are also families who do have cousins named Christopher Michael and Christopher John. Try to get a different perspective. Maybe SHE named all her dolls Chris and Chrissy. Again, life is too short. Let it go.

Don't Do It, Girlfriend

Think about how hurt and horrified you would be if a relative or close friend stole your baby-to-be's name. Or worse, your name. Make sure that you don't steal anyone else's idea, either. There are too many nice names to fight over one. And it's so much more fun to find that one perfect name, and make your sister faint with envy.

We Haven't Picked a Name Yet

Having someone steal the name is one of the pitfalls of not reserving the name first. It still is the way that I always went. It's fun to make everyone wait. Keep 'em guessing. Don't even announce the sex.

You will be amazed at how many conversations they can have about whether it's a girl or a boy. If you tell the name before the birth, someone will inevitably crush you with criticism. Or yawn and sniff with boredom because yeah, yeah, you ALREADY told us that Jeremiah Josiah Joshua Jones was coming on November 26.

Here Comes the Baby!

If you announce the name after Baby arrives, everyone will be too busy cooing over those cute little baby toes and that sweet baby nose to hurt your feelings. But who cares, as long as we all love the baby. And . . . you can't call it "It" forever. Or "The Baby," or "Soooooo Cute." Not forever, really.

The Dos and Don'ts of Naming

A Family Name

Think about your last name. Some families have one last name, the old-fashioned way. It is often quite lovely for everyone in the family to share one common name. The feminist rulebook actually doesn't rule out taking the father's name only. And if it did, remember that, when passing on the mother's last name, it was often passed on to her from, you guessed it, another guy—her father. So, if you are passing on only one last name, you just have to find one great first name, and maybe one great middle name, to go with your last name. Sounds easy? Sometimes it is.

The Hyphen Department

But some families (and you know who you are) have two or three last names. Maybe that's the family name, or maybe you just haven't had to decide which name or names you're going to use, until now. Well, now you're committed. So figure it out. Which name goes first? What sounds best? Are you going to use hyphens, or not? If not, does the first of your last names become the baby's middle name? Will you name every one of your children with those two names?

Now it gets complicated. Some families use the mother's last name as the middle name, and the father's last name as the last name for their sons. They use the father's last name as the middle name, and the mother's last name as the last name for their daughters. Are you still following this? Will anyone else be able to follow this? This means that the siblings may or may not have the same last name as each other and their parents. Will your child feel part of the Smith family if her last name is Jones?

In this day and age of families and stepfamilies, you can see how the hyphen thing can get out of hand. Imagine the complications if your friends wanted to invite your whole family to a wedding. What exactly should it say on the invitation? The Needleson-Alejandro-Fokerstein Family, plus Sven and Tomiko?

So, if you were planning to give this child two or three last names, with hyphens, it may be time to think again. What will happen a few generations down the road? Remember, if Sebastian Seymour Lipshitz-Finklestein grows up to marry Marie-Chantal Solange Blossom Golbergstine-Kennedy-Andropolousian, then imagine the possibilities of their grandchildren's names. What will the towel monograms say? Yeesh.

Be aware that, even in this day and age of diversity and understanding, the other kids at school will call your whole family by the dad's last name. It's just too complicated that Mr. Smith's wife is Dr. Jones; it's inevitable that they will call her Mrs. Smith anyway. Simplify that last name, if you can. Or, imagine the complications. And, once you know what the baby's last name is, you can get down to business, and find a first name that blends perfectly.

The End of the Line

It's a shame when a lovely family last name dies out. But, if you have a great last name, like Parker, it could work as a first name. Your problems are solved! Names like Morgan, Blakely, Cameron, and Williams; Everett, Ling, Burke, and Delaney; Mackenzie, Cruz, Jefferson, and Stevens can make great first names. If we're talking about Streitenheimer or Haseenfeffer, forget about it.

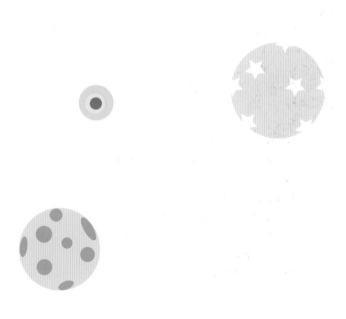

Family Name Traditions

Welcome to the World, Baby Mine

Many families carry on a tradition of having a baby naming. You will hear the name announced officially for the first time at a christening, baptism, bris, or naming ceremony. Sometimes it is in a house of worship, sometimes at home. Religion may be a big part of the day, mentioned briefly, or not included. Even if it's not your custom to officially welcome Baby to the world, maybe it should be. There is no better excuse in the world for a party. It's time to start your own, new, lovely traditions.

Think about the naming traditions in your families. Some have the custom of naming the first boy after Daddy, and the second after Grandpa and Pop Pop. After that, the next five boys get the uncles' names. There are a lot of minefields here. Many families have one or two children. And some children have four or five grandfathers. And you may not want to honor only a few relatives, and hurt others by leaving them out. Or you adore some of the uncles much more than others. You might end up having to use a name you don't really love. And you never get to pick a name you do love.

Are you sure you have such a strong family tradition that you will be officially Out-of-the-Will if you don't use the name Eliott Windsor Wadsworth Rockingham-Jones?

Stepping Carefully with Stepparents

Sometimes, you have to tippytoe carefully if your stepfather was more a part of your life than your father was. Or there are two Gilberts, one of whom is really nice, the other not so much. If feelings could be hurt in any way, don't name the baby after anybody.

Names Honoring Those Who Have Passed On

Some families follow the tradition of naming a child after a relative who has passed away. This is a very sweet idea, but can be painful if the loss is recent. Sometimes it's touching to have the name live again. Other times it's just too sad, and can hurt your heart all day long. One solution is to name the child in remembrance of the deceased; thus, changing the name, and leaving the sentiment. You could call her Emma Lynn, or even Emmilyn, and remember both Grandma Edna and Grandma Lucretia, thus making everyone happy.

How clever you are! You honored the family, and Baby still ends up with a lovely, unique, and modern name. And you can still pass on those monogrammed hankies and engraved lockets. You even graciously left room for your sisters to name their babies after the grandmas, too. And, everyone will be soooo glad to remember how much we adored our two funny grandmas.

If you're not really naming that baby Ethelbert to get your mitts on the family silver, and I hope you're not, you can also consider using Great-Grandma or Great-Grandpa's name as a middle name.

Too Many Alistairs

Also, it gets a bit of the Department of Redundancy Department if there are just a few too many Fredericks on both sides. Nice, but Thanksgiving and the family barbeque end up packed with eleven males having the same name. It cuts time when you call everyone for dinner. Holler, "Frederick!" and they'll all come running, but do you really want that? Try telling a story about how cute it was when Frederick took Frederick and little Frederick to play baseball. But Frederick had a cold and couldn't come. And WHO was on first?

Tony, Cousin Tony, and His Brother, Tony

If you still love the tradition of giving Baby a family name, but see that messy mess of having multiple cousins named Floyd and Jessamyn, consider using the same name over and over, but giving each child a variation as the official nickname. There are lots of Williams in my mother's family, and my father's, too. You might think about naming the baby William, but calling him Bill or Billy or Willie or Wolfie. Then, there's room at the table for your grandsons to be all Williams, and be called Bubba, Wilkie-Wils, Liam, Wilson, and Gillie. Even granddaughter, little Wilhelmena and Cousin Willow. You can get a lot of mileage out of the name William. You won't even have to stretch to Guillermo, Wilhelm, or the dreaded Gwilyam.

Godparents

Many people have the custom of asking friends or relatives to be the baby's godparents. These people are often entrusted with the responsibility of carrying on religious or family traditions. And, if the unthinkable happens, to step in when the parents aren't there. Many parents carry the honor further by naming the baby after a godparent; first name, middle name, or initial. This custom carries the same honors and pitfalls of naming the baby after anyone else.

Honor Your Nationality

What's not American about a kid named Sushi? You can honor your nationality by giving your child a name that gives just a sweet nod to your heritage. For example, instead of naming a little girl Altheda or Theaphania, name her Theodora and call her Thea. Everyone in America can say it, spell it, and get it, and it still says that you are Greek and proud of it. And everyone in the neighborhood will love the name, not just those from the old country.

Little Masako will not appreciate her name if all the other girls in ballet class are named Mary and Priscilla. You could consider calling her Alexandra Masako. She will have the option of using either name, or both, at any time in her life.

How to Honor the Family, and the Baby, Too

Junior Junior The Third Redux

If you gotta gotta name the baby after Daddy, consider giving him a different middle name, or at least a different nickname. Just beware of Tommy and little Thomas and big Thomas. And now we all know little Thomas, who is taller than big Thomas, but not as tall as his cousin Thomas Junior Junior the Third, also known as Tom, the father of Tommy. And on it goes.

One-Twenty-sixth of the Alphabet

You can also honor the family by giving Baby a unique and pretty name by using a first initial only. You can just go through all the R's or X's in the book. Or, you can creatively change Uncle Ethyl's name to little Eliot. Everyone will love the sentiment, and little Eliot won't have to start therapy at three.

First and Last Name Tips

Length

Try to give a short first name with a really long last one, and vice versa. Maryrose Smythe sounds better than Maryrose Hamilton-Silverberg-Jones. And looks better, too.

Names that Smoosh Together

Think about the sounds that connect both names. Susan Nass is sure to be called Susan Ass her whole life. James Sweeney will be thought of as James Weenie. Cross name combinations like these out, and look for another.

Sounds Wrong

Alliteration either works, or it doesn't. Lucie Little is sweet, Michael Morgan works, but Zachary Zanadoo is just wrong.

Picking That Perfect Name

Some parents really want to wait until the baby is born before choosing a name. Okay, this is fine, but I suggest you agree on a short list of little pink names and little blue names before the big day. You don't want to make a choice you'll regret because you are so happy that you're not paying attention. Or so tired, or filled with adrenaline that you'll cave.

Find some names you love, any one of which you both would be thrilled to name your little one. Then, when Baby comes, you can close your eyes and point at the list, flip a coin, or let that little baby face tell you what fits. There, you can't go wrong. You don't need to take a poll. Or ask strangers in the street. You can do this. And you don't have to wait until little Sugarbabyhoneysnookieookums can talk to help you decide.

Are You a Girl, or Are You a Boy?

Never, ever, ever give a boy a girl's name. I forbid it. Your son will never forgive you.

You can give a girl a boy's name, but it's best to do it as a nickname. Then, she can have the option of being Michael, or switching back to Michaela; and Stevie can return to Stephanie.

As enlightened as we think we are in this day and age, try to give a daughter a girly name, and a son a masculine one. It is awful to go through life trying to correct everyone's assumptions about you. Don't get too cute with spelling, either. It's a total pain to slowly spell your name every time you use a credit card. It's enough of a burden to go through junior high school, without the added burden of a weird name. Stick with the classics, and you can't go wrong, baby.

A cautionary tale: Very early one school year, I was planning my child's birthday party. Invitations were about to be mailed to all the boys in the grade, including the new boy, Jackson. Luckily, I found out just in time that Jackson was the new girl. The prospect of embarrassing her, and her parents, mortified me. Until that moment, I always thought unisex names and boys' names for girls were cute. This is a perfect example of the misunderstandings these children can encounter for a lifetime.

How Trendy is Too Trendy?

Here's another tightrope you must walk: giving your tiny one a name that is normal, sweet-sounding, and average. Nothing to tease about. Trendy, but not too trendy. Filled with promise, just like Baby. But yet, who can foresee that there will be eleven Dantes in the seventh grade? And yet you must.

I thought that I was so very clever to call my first son Benjamin, a lovely, normal, Biblical name. Oooo, still oh-so unusual, since it was still being used by the grandpa set. You cannot imagine how many Benjamins came out in 1982. Oh, well. I still love the name, and adore that my father's and uncle's names are constantly honored by Ben. And he would prefer to be Ben Z. forever, rather than anything else. My other boys have pretty common names: Daniel, Michael, and the ubiquitous William. But we lucked out. These names were not as common as a lot of others those years. So you just never know.

23

Once in a While, You Just Get Lucky

If meanings are important to you, you will have to eliminate some perfectly yummy names. But, sometimes the whole meaning thing works by accident. Phoebe and Melanie, both Greek names, mean light and dark. But, more importantly, they sound so right together, and I don't know why. Very pretty and feminine, and sing-songy. But they don't rhyme. So good together. So are Zoë and Eve, both meaning life. From two different languages, Greek and Hebrew. But they just work.

Perfect

You want a lovely, accepted name for the baby. Trust me, you do. Something instantly recognizable, classic, and proper. A name that won't get your child's application for the perfect college or job tossed because the powers-that-be assume little Radiohead or Sxiiemp is a little too wacky, and not our kind, dear.

Now, just to make you run screaming into the night and give up, you have to have the perfect, classic name, but not the dreaded flavor of the year. You might not know this until first grade, and it might be traumatic to change little Sophie or Stephan's name at this late date.

I once witnessed two out-of-control boys in the sandbox, whose nannies were too busy chatting to do any nannying. I called out for Andrew's grown-up. E.S.P.? I think not. I just knew that the chances were great that one of those boys was Andrew that year.

Pay attention to what names are on the pile of birth announcements you haven't had time to buy gifts for. You might just see some patterns emerging. If you use your radar, you may be able to anticipate the Year of the Tiffanys, or the Montanas, Morgans, Bostons, Nildas, Omars, Celadines, Apples, Peachies, Rubys, or Pixies. But chances are, you won't.

In choosing a name, sometimes you just have to wing it. When I chose my kids' names, I was lucky, and maybe a little smart. You just have to guess. And trust your instincts. Little Violet or Malcolm will love you no matter what.

You Better Love that Name Now, or You'll Be Sorry

Say each name out loud, a whole bunch of times. You will not believe how many times you need to say Max, Max, Maaaaaax! in the course of a day. Make sure you really love the name, If anything irritates you about it this early in the game, move on.

How Do You Spell that Again?

Always use the proper and classic spelling of a name. It will save time and aggravation for years to come if people just know how to spell it, pronounce it, and get it. It's Christopher, not Krisstufuh, Krysterfyre, or Creestoofr. Just Christopher.

What were Your Parents Thinking?

You just don't want to attach a bad label to a kid, and it is exhausting for a child to explain how to spell the name, or why your parents named you Gamma or Fredith. Over and over again. How hideous to go through life trying to explain that it's Gwilyme, not William. Most boys would rather be plain old Billy. Give the kid a break.

Creative, not Kooky

If you love the name, but feel like there might be too many little Nicoles at kindergarten, how about Nicolette or Nicoline? Just don't go too far out, and call her Neiquitetta. Turn James into Jameson, but skip Jaquariuan.

Double First Names

Just to make things more complicated, now that you've decided on Jane or John, you can double up first names. Peggy Sue, Maryanne, Ricki Jo, Amberose, and Anna-Mae are all fun names. John Henry is great, but not Billybob Dickie. Get the picture?

Parlez-vous Français?

French names sometimes mix genders, but the gender of the child being named comes first. Thus, Jeanne-Michel is a girl, and Pierre-Michelle is a boy. This still could be confusing for many people, so only use a combination like this if it is your family tradition. Otherwise, Stéphane and Mereille are perfectly perfect, and just French enough.

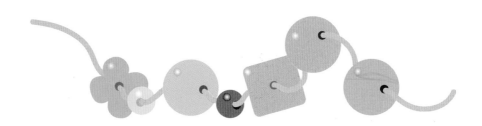

There are Never Enough Marys

If you are creative, the possibilities can go on and on. My cousins named every girl Mary, with another name tacked on. There's Mary Rose, Mary Katherine, Mary Sophie, and Mary Claire. Each girl is called by her second name.

Religion

There are plenty of mainstream names that are in holy books. Stories from your religion are packed with saints and true heroes and heroines with excellent names. Do your homework. Make sure you are naming your baby after someone with a great story. Little Isaac or Mohammed will thank you some day.

Pronunciation

If you're not sure how a name is pronounced, then chances are that the rest of the world will be confused, too. Is Gisela, "Gee-seh-la," or "Juh-sel-la?" Uh. Better switch to Giselle or Gabriella. Ask a random three-year-old to pronounce the whole name. Tell your nephew Sherman all three names. Just say it once, and ask him to say it, too. If he says, something unintelligible, maybe you'd better go back to the list, and simplify it a bit.

ABC, Easy as 1, 2, 3

Your kids don't have to be born in alphabetical order. If you name your children Adam, Barbara, Clarissa, David, Evelyn, Fabiana, and George, you are silly.

Color Names

I love color names. Violet is my favorite color, and a damned fine name to boot. Also, Ione, Gray, Lavender, and Lilac. Red is a nickname, but only if your kid's friends give it to him. Blue is not a name, but a sweet middle name, boy or girl. There's Saffron, Coral, Peachy, and Blanca. And Rose, what could be sweeter? You wouldn't name her Yellow, but how cute is Xanthe or Sunny?

Flower and Gem Names

Little girls with flowery names: Rosie, Lily, Daffodil, Hyacinth, Poppy, Daisy, and the always adorable Violet. How delightful . . . and their cousins, Ruby, Sapphire, Opal, and Jade.

Overdoing Cute

Delicious little names, like color, flower, and gem ones, can be overdone. Stick to one, and give the other siblings equally wonderful names that mean something else.

Names to Skip Over Right Away

Remember, be gracious, and eliminate any names that your relatives have already used. Ditto for close friends and movie stars.

What Were You Thinking

A fellow mother at nursery school unconsciously (I think, I hope) gave her children the names of the kids on the Brady Bunch. Luckily, she broke the pattern with number five.

Ruined Names

There are perfectly wonderful names that are so over-identified with an incredibly famous, or infamous person, that you just can't use them. If this person is a criminal, rock star, character on a classic television program, or your town drunk, the name may be ruined for you, and your child may have trouble escaping the association later. Too much to live up to, or too much to live down. There's no getting around it. Just cross it off the list, and keep searching.

Famous Names

And I forbid you to name your child after a famous store, or any avenue in any big city. Or a tree or a fruit. Names like Cherry or Berry should be reserved for nicknames. Not after any character on television who is the first one to pop in one's mind when it's said out loud, thank you.

Adopted Kids

It doesn't matter if that child grew in your belly or in your heart, this is your little love. Give all your kids the most wonderful names in the world. Like any group of siblings, give them fabulous, normal names that go together.

If the child was adopted from a different country, some parents may wish to give a name that honors the tradition of that country. If you live in a place where lots of other little kids will have similar names, by all means do it. Another solution would be to give a mainstream first name, and a middle name of Ling or Nikita or Pablo. This is also a wonderful solution for families who straddle two cultures.

Make-believe Names

Don't do it. It's not cute, trendy, or nice. Just weird. Same with make-believe spelling.

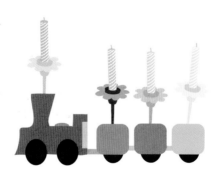

Old-fashioned Names

Sometimes names come back in style. Many others should stay in ancient history. Samuel and Nathaniel, Duncan and Daniel are lovely. So are Melissa and Alexandra and Tessa. I think we can say goodbye to Ethel and Clem, Marvin and Bertha. Cleopatra is hideous. Cleo is delicious. So are Clea and Thea, Patsy and Bess.

Girly Girls, and Manly Men

It seems okay to give girls sweet, girly names, but boys need classic, masculine, somewhat ordinary names. Thus, the proliferation of Lilys and Daisies and Sophies, playing with Edwards and Michaels, and Toms. Name your girl after a flower, gem, or most upper-class Brits, and I melt. Name her Bambi or Pebbles, Tinky or Muffie, I gag. It's a bad, bad thing.

Nicknames and Initials

Thomas John Astor Duke III can be called T. J., or Trey (the third), Tom, Tommy, or Tad. He also has a lot of places to go if he later feels his original nickname is babyish. Fergus Leo Ephraim Potage is just stuck. Patricia Iris Galen's classmates will figure her initials out in five minutes. Don't do it. Ditto for Yacov Uriah Kent. Yours and Mine are not real names. Neither are Teetee, Zuzu, Popo, Iggy, Piggy, Moonbeam, and Stinky. Weezie, Poodle Pie, Muffy, and Pebbles are nicknames. Nicknames, I say!

Changing That Name

There is a playground song that goes:

I hate my name, I'm gonna throw it in the Atlantic Ocean, I hate
my name, oh I hate my name. I'm gonna throw it away . . .

I know lots of grown-ups who have changed their names, for lots of reasons. Just none that I really thought was worth having thirty years' worth of friends and relatives rolling their eyes, shrugging, and saying, "huh?" for. I have four friends who changed their children's names after their first birthdays. I don't think it's such a common practice, I may just have some um, creative friends.

Be aware that it's a big deal to change a name legally. Sometimes red tape at the birth certificate place and the passport office takes a year to get everything changed, and they may not come back to you so fast. So, don't plan that trip to Paris, or get in line to register for kindergarten, until you figure it out. It also may be very confusing to the child to be called Felicia until six, then Rosalie after that.

Anticipating Siblings to Be

Siblings (especially multiples) should have names that blend beautifully. Ben and Noah; and Rebecca, Jessica, and Rosie-Lee are just perfect. So are Joseph and Melody; Lucie and Lilac; Esmé and Violet. How sweet. Moe, Larry, and Curly should be reserved for the cats. Sibling names should be unique, yet somehow work together. It's hard to anticipate this before your first child is even born, but you must. If you use Sam for your first, be prepared to cross Pam, Stan, Sandy, and Jan off your list in the future.

I made a list for my first child, and put the names in order of those I loved, loved, loved. Every time another baby was on the way, I poured over the name books, spending hours dreaming of cute, artsy names. And I always came back to the same names on the first list. In order, one, two, three, four, five. And I still adore each name, all these years later.

Do these names sound great together? Do they make sense? Whether they're triplets, or five years apart, Gwendolyn, Genevieve, and Guinevere will make you the laughing stock of the PTA crowd. And everyone will be looking for Gwyneth.

So, what do you look for when planning out sibling names that sound right together? What really works are names that have the same syllables, but please no rhyming! It's too, too tacky to be the mother of Barry, Sari, Larry, Harry, and Carrie. Any questions?

If so, see the sibling section for more tips, and some pretty cute combinations.

Sibling Rivalry

It's bad enough that you are bringing home a littler, cuter version of your beloved first child. Just imagine if your husband brought home a littler, cuter version of you. And she didn't have to do any of the work, just look cute. And you had to run around and share your stuff and get her clean underwear. Good grief. So, don't add insult to injury and make the mistake of offering little Seymour the honor of naming the new baby—and then having to take it back, because he wants to name his sister Satan. Why are you surprised?

Family friends back in the '50s did exactly that, and ended up with a little girl named Dale. Quite sweet, but her brother insisted that he was promised he could name her anything he wanted. And that would be Roy Rogers. Evans forbid, he might have chosen Trigger. So, think long and hard before you make an offer like this. Unless you don't mind being the parents of Randall, Rocky, and Bullwinkle.

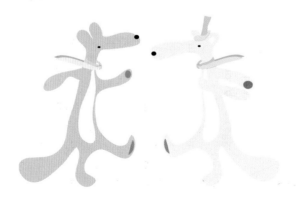

Sibling Name Tips

Repeating Letters

Lottie, Lucinda, Ludie, Larry, Lancelot, Louis, Lucky, and Lulu. All great names, but not for one family. Do you really want to be known as the Elles family?

And, Speaking of "J" Names

With the stroller crowd, you will notice multitudes of little Jakes, Jodies, Jessicas, Jacks, Jadens, and Julies. Jennifers, Juliets, JJs, Jeffs, and Jeds. For some reason, for years actually, names starting with the letter "J" have been a little overdone. What's up with that?

Siblings Names that Fall Over Each Other Trying Too Hard

You just can't have three girls named Madison, Magdalene, and Madeline. Or Jonas, Jonah, and Jonesey. You will spend so much time with your children that you will know every freckle. This isn't the case with the rest of the world. Nobody's going to ask your kids to that birthday party if they're too hard to tell apart; if they look alike and have the same first names, trust me, it ain't great.

When Every Day is Pay-Attention-to-Me-Day

I once knew identical twin girls; one named Belinda, who wore short hair with bangs and a barrette every day. Her sister, Pamela, had long plaits. I know, their description sounds like something straight out of the old jump rope song, "A, My Name is Alice . . . " But this mother was really quite brilliant to give her girls separate identities and visual clues to help others see them as two unique people. Good mothering, I say.

Anagrams

Siblings with names that are anagrams–like Amy and May, Vera and Reva, Myra and Mary–will grow up to punish you. Don't do it. No. no, never, never. And if you do, don't say I didn't warn you.

Starts with the Letter

As with any siblings, don't go overboard with using the same letter over and over. Maisie and Marigold can be cute; Owen and Olive are not. Nanette, Naomi, and Nicholas are trying too hard. Everyone's tongues will be twisted trying to say, "hello."

Mirror Names

Reversing the letters is a wolf cry to the bullies. Come tease my babies. So skip Nadia and Aidan; Ira and Ari.

Double Meanings

Cute meanings don't mean much to anyone else. Paloma, Jemima, and Columba all mean "dove," but don't sound that great together.

Pete and Repeat: Twins, Triplets, and More

Everything mentioned above about the pitfalls of naming siblings, goes double and triple for multiples. At the risk of repeating myself (sorry, bad pun) I repeat: Give each multiple a unique and beautiful name, as if they were siblings of different ages. Using names with the same first initials can work sometimes, but it often just makes it that much harder for others to remember which one is which. Don't dress them alike, don't name them alike. They're twins, they're cute–we get it.

The names must go together, but not too much. Same number of syllables is good (Peter and Thomas); rhyming is bad (Annie and Fanny). Do you love charming, old-fashioned names? Give each multiple one. Don't mix Dorothy with Tiffany.

Name multiples with names from the same country. Ahmet and Nasir are great; Avi and Ahmad not so much. Feel free to break this rule if your family background reflects two different cultures.

Try out the multiple combinations backward and forward. Make sure they don't accidentally have the same names as someone famous, or worse, infamous. So that rules out Bonnie and Clyde, Wilma and Fred, Adam and Eve, Sonny and Cher. Fred and Ethel, Lucy and Ethel, Lucy and Ricky, Lucy and Desi.

Names that have similar meanings can accidentally sound amazing together, like Pearl and Pegeen, but not Flora and Fleur. How about Violet, Ione, and Lilac? Just don't go overboard and name your second set of triplets Lavender, Rose, and let's see . . . Orange?

1 2 3 4 5 6 7 8

Middle Name Muddles

Are you kidding me? I have to find a middle name? Now that you are totally overwhelmed, remember that you may need to find a middle name for this child. Is this important? I'm not sure.

Use the Middle Name First

It is actually a wonderful thing to have a middle name. If you simply cannot live with your first name, you can drop it, and there is a perfectly lovely name just waiting to be used.

Some parents opt to skip the middle name. You can leave it blank forever, or let little Axelrod or Hermione fill in the blank later. Just make sure that you put a dash in the blank of the birth certificate form, or your child may be named Stuart None Fast, Noah No Norris, or Elodie Blank LeBlanc.

Phoney Baloney Middle Names

None of my four boys has a middle name. But every once in a while, you need to say both names to get their attention. Even more alarmingly, all three. So, I later gave each of them the middle name Carter. Now, not on their birth certificates or passports, mind you. Just out loud when I mean business. It works surprisingly well. And every once in a while, I change that middle name. Just to keep them on their toes, and see if they're really listening. Use this method sparingly for maximum effectiveness.

Changing the Middle Name Later

A word of caution: Do not let the child change a name officially until adulthood. An eleven-year-old may just love the name Batman or Dog-Doggy-Dog, but live to regret it ten years later. I even had one child who gave himself Bart (as in Simpson) as a middle name for all of third grade. The teacher never knew.

You Can Always Use Vanderbilt or Roosevelt

If you get really stuck, there are plenty of all-purpose middle names. Rose, Jane, Carter, and Joseph go with lots of names. So do Michael, Daniel, Mary, Anne, Smith, Blue, and Farley. Even Simpson. You'll be fine.

The Initial Instead of a Middle Name

Lots of letters can be used instead of a middle name. Harry Truman had one. Just be careful of naming your child Alfred D. Maus, or Johnny B. Goode, or Ina (I.) P. Dailey.

Made-up and Throw-away Middle Names

An old friend named her final child "Thendolyne" because she was the end of the line. If you must be cute and creative, do it with the middle name. It's there forever, satisfying you, and your child can spend a lifetime never ever saying it out loud.

That Twinkle in Your Eye

When you first see your baby, your heart will stop for a moment, and the earth will stand still. It doesn't matter if it is summer, winter, fall, or spring. You'll be chilled, and you won't be able to breathe, yet you'll be crying and laughing. Oh, what a beautiful morning, oh, what a beautiful day. This little one who wasn't here five minutes ago looks nothing like you imagined for all those nine months. Yet strangely familiar. Who is this person? That funny, slippery, screechy little thing really looks just like your wrinkled uncle. Or maybe Winston Churchill. Pretty gorgeous, don't you think? Like a little fuzzy kitten. Maybe you better pick a couple of names soon . . . now . . . before the baby comes. Your emotions might get the best of you, and you could end up with a baby named King Charles the First. Or Miss Trixie-Pixiepie Kewpiedoll Angelface Pussycat Mine.

Now Find It! The Perfect Name

So, what are you waiting for? You can cherish the sentiment of naming this child after someone you love, or have loved. Or name it after nobody at all. Whatever you decide, it's gonna be great.

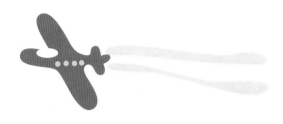

How to Use the Name Listings

The greatest gift you can give Baby is a nice, normal, slightly unusual, totally cool, and perfect name. Something just right that Baby can easily grow into. Finding a brand new name for a brand new baby is the best. Sometimes it's just fun to check out what names mean and see if someone's name matches his or her personality. Or appearance. Or not.

There are two main lists in this book—girls and boys. Each name is accompanied by its origin (if known) and meaning. Some name entries mention famous people who share that name, and nicknames and endearments.

Definitions: My Name Means WHAT?

For some parents the definition of a name is deeply important; for others it has little meaning. Many people have long and marvelous lives and couldn't care less what their names mean. It's still pretty charming to look up YOUR name, and see that, indeed, you are strong and brilliant, and come from the deep forest.

Origins

Names you thought were 100 percent American might have ancient roots in another culture. Many English names clearly come from the

Old Latin. Other names have unclear origins. Then there are names that spill over from one geographic region to the next.

Our country is a fabulous melting pot where different is often more interesting. It's not uncommon to find Keisha, May-Ling, Allesandra, and Jennifer playing with Ephraim, Osgood, Killian, Seiji, and José. A name might have more resonance for you if it is a Scottish name, and your grandparents came from Scotland. But don't let it stop you if your family has no connection to the country of origin. If the name sounds mainstream American to you, it probably is.

It's nice to have a general knowledge of the origin of a name, and the meaning, too, but the most important task is to pick that great name. That's the one thing your little one carries around forever.

Trust Your First Instinct

You might find a name or two on this list that you never, ever thought of. And fall in love. Or, you might have chosen the perfectly perfect name in the third grade. Or, perhaps you always knew that you would have babies named Adeline, Barney, Franklin, and Sue.

Scribble a list of names that tickle you as you read this book. The name will come to you; I promise. It was there all along. Lightning will strike you, and there will only be one perfect name for little Theo or Archibald or Pegeen.

There it is. The perfect name. And you'll know. It wasn't Christopher after all. It was little Clarissa or Noriko or Addison or Charles. Or Harper or Ahmed or Tucker or Mary Ashlyn or Joe. Abbie or Xanthe or Ruby or Phillipe.

Your very own best loved name. See? It was there all along.

Girls' Names

Abbie a short form of Abigail.

Abbott Hebrew: a father.

Abigail Hebrew: a father's delight. **Abbie, Abby, Abi.**

Acacia Greek: thorny; from the acacia tree.

Acadia French: a place in Nova Scotia, Canada.

Ada Saxon: festive; wealthy. **Addie, Addy, Aida, Eda, Edith, Ida.**

Addison Saxon: offspring of Adam.

Addy a short form of Ada. **Addie.**

Adelaide Saxon: dignified and of a generous nature. **Adele, Adela, Adelia, Adeline.**

Adele a short form of Adelaide. **Adela, Della, Adeline, Adelaide.**

Adina Hebrew: tender; subtle; a feminine form of Adin. **Adeana.**

Adora Saxon: one who is loved and admired.

Adriana a form of Adrienne. **Adrianna.**

Adrienne Latin: a female from the ocean; a feminine form of Adrian. **Adrienna, Adria, Adriana, Adrianna.**

Afton English: from the town of Afton.

Agatha Greek: fine. Agatha Christie, British author. **Agathe, Aggie.**

Agnes Greek: wholesome; innocent; tender. **Agnella, Nessie, Neysa, Anesse, Agna.**

Aimee French: one who is loved. **Aimée, Amy.**

Ainsley Scottish and English: transferred use of a surname; refers to a forest and a hermitage. **Ainslee.**

Aisha Arabic: animate and happy; to live.

Aisling a form of Ashling.

Ala Arabic: rise; distinction; preeminence; to go up.

Alana Celtic: fine-looking or attractive; a feminine form of Alan. **Alanna, Elana, Alina, Helen, Lana, Lane.**

Alberta Saxon: dignified and bright; a feminine form of Albert. **Albertine, Albertina, Berta, Bertie, Bert.**

Alden English: a wise protector.

Aleeka Nigerian: a little girl who drives out a beautiful woman.

Aleela African: she who cries.

Alessandra a form of Alexandra.

Alessia a form of Alice.

Alex a short form of Alexandra.

Alexa a short form of Alexandra.

Alexandra Greek: one who helps humanity; a feminine form of Alexander. Tsarina Alexandra, German-born last Empress of Russia. **Alex, Alix, Allie, Ally, Ali, Alexis, Alexa, Lexi, Alexandria, Alexandre, Alexandrie, Alessandra, Sandy, Sandi, Sandra, Sondra, Alondra, Sasha, Sascha.**

Alexandre a form of Alexandra. **Alexandrie.**

Alexis a form of Alexandra. **Lexi.**

Alia Arabic: to rise up. **Alya, Alyah.**

Alice Saxon: reality; dignified; a shortened form of the ancient name, Adeliz. Alice, fictional heroine of Lewis Carroll's *Alice's Adventures in Wonderland and Through the Looking Glass*. **Alyce, Alicia, Alison, Elissa, Alyssa, Alessia, Elsie.**

Alicia a form of Alice. **Alisha, Elisha.**

Alison a form of Alice. **Allison.**

Alma Latin: treasured; caring; compassionate; abundant.

Alodie English: wealthy.

Alondra Spanish: a form of Alexandra.

Althea Greek: pure; curing. **Thea, Altheta.**

Alyssa a form of Alice. **Elissa.**

Amabel French: loveable and beautiful.

Amalie a form of Emily. Amalie Freud, Sigmund's mommy.

Amanda Latin: endearing. **Mandy.**

Amanda Jane a combination of Amanda and Jane.

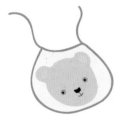

Amaryllis Greek: refreshing and sparkling; a form of a lily; common name of a shepherd girl or country girl in classical pastoral poetry; including Virgil's *Eclogues*.

Amber Arabic: a jewel. **Amberlyn.**

Ambrosia Greek: eternal; something extremely pleasing to taste or smell. **Ambrose, Amberose.**

Amelia Saxon: hard-working; determined; a feminine form of Emil. Amelia Earhart, American aviatrix. **Amélie, Melia, Mell, Millie.**

Amelinda a form of Emily and Linda.

Amena Celtic: truthful.

Ames English: transferred use of a surname.

Amethyst Greek: a purple crystallized stone.

Amity Latin: camaraderie; charity.

Amory Latin: to be in love with.

Amy a form of Aimee. Amy, littlest of four March sisters in Louisa May Alcott's *Little Women*; her name is an anagram of May. **Aimée.**

Anabel Latin: loveable and beautiful. **Anabelle, Amabel.**

Anäis Catalan and Hebrew: graceful; gracious. Anäis Nin, French-born author.

Ananda Sanskrit: glee; pleasure.

Anastasia Greek: a person who will rise again; rebirth. Anastasia Romanov, the youngest Grand Duchess of Russia. **Ana, Anastasie, Stacey, Stacy.**

Anatole Greek: from the East.

Andrea Italian: feminine; a feminine form of Andrew. **Andi, Andie, Andrée, Drea.**

Anemone Greek: an herb in the buttercup family with showy flowers.

Anesse a form of Agnes.

Angela Greek: celestial herald; beatific. **Angel, Angeline, Angelina, Angelena, Angelita, Angelica, Angelique, Angie, Lena.**

Angelica a form of Angela.

Angelina Italian: a form of Angela. **Angelena, Angeline, Lena, Angel, Leenie.**

Angeline a form of Angela.

Angelique French: a form of Angela.

Anica Swedish: a form of Ann. **Annika.**

Anita Hebrew: elegance. **Anitra.**

Ann Hebrew: full of blessings and compassion. **Anne, Annie, Ani, Anna, Ana, Anica, Annika, Anushka, Nan, Nancy, Nanon, Nanette.**

Anna a form of Ann. **Ana.**

Annamaria a combination of Anna and Maria.

Annamay a combination of Ann and May. **Annamae.**

Annelise a form of Anne and Lisa. **Anelise.**

Annette French: a favor. Annette Funicello, American Mousketeer and actress. **Netty, Nettie.**

Annice Greek: completion.

Annmarie a form of Ann and Marie. **Annamaria.**

Annora a form of Honor.

Anouk Czech: a form of Anushka. Anouk Aimée, French actress.

Anthea Greek: flower-like. **Bluma, Flora, Fleur, Thea.**

Antoinette Latin: exceedingly wonderful; a flower; feminine form of Anthony. Marie Antoinette, 18th-century queen of France. **Antonia, Netta, Nettie, Toinette, Toni.**

Antonia a form of Antoinette.

Anushka Czech: a form of Ann. Anoushka Hempel, British designer. **Anoushka, Anouska, Anouk.**

Anya Russian: a form of Hannah.

Appolonia Greek: from the sun god, Apollo. **Apollonia, Apollinaria.**

April Latin: to open; a spring month following March and before May. **Averil, Avril.**

Arabella Latin: a light and gorgeous altar. **Arrabelle, Bell, Belle, Bella.**

Araminta English: a name of unknown meaning, popular in 18th-century England. Araminta Ross, real name of Harriet Tubman, runaway slave and heroine of the Underground Railway. **Minty.**

Arden English: from the valley of the eagles.

Ardith Hebrew: a flowering meadow.

Aria Latin: air; a striking melody sung by a solo voice accompanied by an instrument, as in an opera.

Ariadine Greek: the sacred one. **Ariadne, Ariana, Arianne.**

Ariana a form of Ariadine. **Arianna.**

Arianne a form of Ariadine.

Ariel Hebrew: a biblical place; a lion of God. Ariel, Disney cartoon mermaid. **Arielle, Ariella, Ariela.**

Arielle French: a form of Ariel.

Arlene Celtic: a promise. **Arlena, Arlana.**

Arlette French: a feminine form of Charles.

Armande French: a feminine form of Armand.

Armelle French: stone chief; a 6th-century Breton saint.

Arnaude French: a form of the masculine name Arnold.

Arnelle German: an eagle. **Arnella.**

Ashanti Ghanian: the people of Ghana; the language spoken there.

Ashley English: transferred use of a surname meaning ash wood.

Ashling Irish: a dream. **Aisling, Aislinn, Ash.**

Ashlyn a combination of Ashley and Lynn.

Ashton English: from the ash tree farm. **Astin.**

Asia English: the eastern sunrise; also, a very large continental land mass.

Asta Scandinavian: to be devoted to; a shortened form of Astrid. Asta, fox terrier in *The Thin Man* films.

Astra Greek: star-like. Astrea. **Aster.**

Astrid Norse: godly power. **Asta.**

Athena Greek: wise person. **Athene.**

Aubrey French: elf power; in German mythology this was the name borne by the elf king. **Avery.**

Auburn Latin: a reddish-brown color.

Auden English: transferred use of a surname meaning friend; British poet W. H. Auden. **Audie.**

Audra a form of Audrey.

Audreen a form of Audrey.

Audrey English: gracious might. **Audra, Audreen, Audria, Audie, Dee.**

Audria a form of Audrey.

August Latin: awe-inspiring; holy. **Augusta, Auguste, Augustina, Augustine, Gussie, Gusta, Tina.**

Augustine a form of August.

Aurelia Latin: small gold-hued woman. **Aurelie, Aurelia, Ora, Oralia, Orel.**

Aurelie a form of Aurelia.

Aurora Latin: the daybreak; the morning; the golden hour. **Aurore.**

Austin English: a contracted form of Augustine; a city in Texas.

Autumn Latin: the season between summer and winter, usually characterized by mild yet crisp weather, and by beautiful foliage.

Ava Greek: a form of Eva.

Avalon Latin: island; also, English: a mythical paradise island to which King Arthur is transported after his death in the English legend of King Arthur.

Aveline Old French: a form of Avis and Eileen.

Averil English: a form of April. Avril Lavigne, Canadian singer. **Avril, Averell**.

Avery French: a form of Aubrey.

Avian Latin: relating to birds.

Avis Latin: a bird. **Ava, Aveline**.

Aviva Hebrew: spring. **Avivi**.

Axelle Scandinavian: a form of Absalom, which is an ancient Hebrew name.

Ayton English: transferred use of a surname.

Azure Persian: a dazzling blue, as the color of the sky or of lapis lazuli.

Babette French: a form of Barbara.

Baby English: a very young child or infant.

Bailey English: transferred use of a surname; a bailiff; a fortified city; a clearing in the woods.

Baines English: transferred use of a surname.

Bambi Italian: child; a shortened form of "bambino." Bambi, Disney cartoon deer.

Bancroft Anglo-Saxon: one who is from the bean field; one who grows beans.

Barbara Greek: mystifying stranger; a person whose origins are not known; a barbarian; eccentric. Barbra Streisand, American singer. **Barbra, Barb, Barbie, Basia, Babs, Babette, Barbette.**

Barclay Scottish: transferred use of a surname; a birch tree clearing.

Barnette French: transferred use of a surname.

Barret English: transferred use of a surname; a quarrel. **Baret.**

Barrie Irish: a form of the masculine name Fionbharr. **Bari.**

Basia Polish: a form of Barbara.

Bayard French: transferred use of a surname.

Beatrice Latin: one who brings happiness. Beatrix Potter, British author. **Bea, Bee, Beatrix, Trixie, Bebe, Bice.**

Bebe Spanish: a form of Beatrice.

Becker English: transferred use of a surname.

Bedelia Irish: strong one.

Belinda Italian: eternal and shrewd. **Bel, Linda, Lindie.**

Belle Italian: a shortened form of Isabella; fine-looking; stunning. **Bella.**

Bernadette Saxon: a mighty and brave person; a feminine form of Bernard. Bernadette Peters, American singer. **Berna, Bernadine, Bernette, Berni.**

Bernice Greek: one who brings happiness. **Berenice, Bernie.**

Bertha German: bright. **Bertrille.**

Bertrille French: a form of Bertha.

Beryl Hebrew: a valuable jewel. **Berry.**

Bess a form of Elizabeth.

Bessie a form of Elizabeth.

Beth Hebrew: house of God.

Bethany Aramaic: a house of figs; the place where Jesus stayed outside of Jerusalem. **Betany, Bethann.**

Bethia a form of Elizabeth.

Betsy a form of Elizabeth.

Bette a form of Elizabeth. Bette Midler, American singer.

Bettiann a form of Elizabeth and Ann.

Bettina a form of Elizabeth.

Betty a form of Elizabeth.

Beulah Hebrew: a person who will be married.

Bevan Irish: a sweet, singing maiden. **Bevin.**

Beverly Anglo-Saxon: a person with great ambition. Beverly Sills, American opera singer. **Bev.**

Bianca Italian: white. Bianca Jagger, Nicaraguan-born social activist. **Blanca**.

Bibi Arabic: a lady; French: a bauble. **Bibiane**.

Bice a form of Beatrice.

Biddy Irish: a form of Bridget.

Bijou French: something very elegant and desired; a dainty jewel. Bijou Phillips, American singer.

Billie Saxon: determination; steadfastness; a shrewd guardian.

Binky Yiddish: a bee; a shortened form of Deborah.

Binnie Celtic: a crib; a wicker basket.

Birdie Old English: a pet form of the word "bird."

Birgitte Swedish: a form of Bridget.

Bitsy English: itsy-bitsy; very small.

Blaine Irish: the thin one.

Blair Scottish: transferred use of a surname; meadow.

Blaise French: lisping; a 4th-century saint.

Blake English: transferred use of a surname; someone with very dark hair.

Blanche French: white; light-skinned; blond. **Branca**, **Blanca**, **Bianca**.

Bliss a form of Blythe.

Blondelle French: blond one.

Blossom Old English: a plant or tree that is in flower. Blossom Dearie, American singer.

Blue English: a color; a state of sadness or melancholy.

Blythe Anglo-Saxon: a happy, mirthful person. Blythe Danner, American actress. **Blithe**, **Bliss**.

Bobbie a form of Roberta.

Bobette a form of Roberta.

Bonita Spanish: a form of Bonnie.

Bonnie Latin: charming; attractive; virtuous. **Bonita**.

Boo English: an interjection used to frighten or startle; a term of endearment.

Booboo English: a term of endearment; a mistake.

Boston English: the capital city of Massachusetts, which was named after a seaport town in England.

Bracie English: a term of endearment.

Brandy Dutch: short for brandywine, a distilled alcoholic beverage made from fruit juice or wine. **Brandi.**

Bree a form of Bridget. **Brie, Brielle.**

Breeze Spanish: a light, gentle wind; one of fair temperament.

Brenda Saxon: a sword; a fiery flame. **Bren, Brennie.**

Brenna Celtic; a maiden with raven-black hair.

Brennie a form of Brenda.

Brett English: transferred use of a surname that originally referred to the Breton people.

Briana English: a feminine form of Brian; high; dignified. **Brianna, Brianne.**

Brianne a form of Briana. **Brianna.**

Brice French: speckled; the name of a 5th-century saint.

Bridget Celtic: fierce; blistering; robust; an ancient Celtic goddess. **Birgitte, Brigid, Biddy, Bridie, Britt, Bree, Brielle.**

Bridie English: a form of Bridget.

Brielle French: a form of Bree.

Britt Swedish: a form of Bridget.

Brittany Latin: from Britain. **Britany, Britney, Britt, Bret, Brita.**

Bronwen Welsh: a pale female breast; sacred. **Bronwyn, Bronnie.**

Brooke Old English: one who dwells by the brook. Brooke Shields, American actress. **Brook, Brookie, Brooks.**

Brookie a form of Brooke.

Brooks a form of Brooke.

Brynn Welsh: hill. **Brynna.**

Bubbles English: a hollow globe, often made of soap and blown as a child's game; a pet name.

Bunny English: a young rabbit; a common diminutive term of endearment for lovers.

C

Cade English: transferred use of a surname. **Cadey.**

Cadence Italian: the modulated rhythm of spoken language, especially poetry, or an inflection in the voice.

Cadey a form of Cade.

Caitlin a form of Katherine.

Calandra Greek: a beauty; a lark. **Callie, Calla, Caley.**

Callie a form of Calandra. **Calla, Caley.**

Callista Greek: the most beautiful. **Calista.**

Camden Scottish: a winding valley.

Cameo Italian: a finely carved precious stone, with different colored layers; a brief, but important part in a play.

Cameron Scottish: transferred use of a surname carried by a well-known Highland clan in Scotland; also, Irish: crooked nose.

Camilla Latin: a noble and righteous handmaiden of unblemished character. **Camille, Cammile, Cammie, Milla, Milly.**

Cammie English: a form of Camilla.

Cammile French: a form of Camilla.

Campbell Scottish: transferred use of a surname carried by a well-known Highland clan in Scotland; also, Irish: crooked mouth.

Candace Latin: glowing; fire-white; pure. Candice Bergen, American actress. **Candy, Candice, Candida, Candy.**

Candide Latin: white; dignity; deliverance.

Caprice Italian: a sudden impulse; a whim.

Cara Celtic: a cherished companion.

Caresse Italian: to touch fondly or affectionately; adore. **Caressa.**

Carina Italian and Scandinavian: a form of Katherine.

Carissa Latin and Greek: dear one; beloved.

Carla Saxon: the strong one; a feminine form of Charles. Carly Simon, American singer. **Carly, Carlie, Karly, Carlyn, Carlin.**

Carlie a form of Carla. **Carly, Karly.**

Carlotta Italian: a form of Charlotte.

Carlyn a form of Carla. **Carlin.**

Carmel Hebrew: the verdant vineyard of God. **Carmella, Carmelita.**

Carmella Hebrew: a garden. **Carmel.**

Carmen Latin: a person related to song or melody. **Carmine, Carmita.**

Carol French: robust and like a woman; a festive song. Carole King, American songwriter and musician. **Carole, Carolina, Carrie, Cary.**

Carola a form of Carolina.

Carolee a combination of Carol and Lee.

Carolina Saxon: resilient; a form of Carol; a feminine form of Charles or Karl. **Carola, Caroline, Carolyn, Line.**

Caroline a form of Carolina. Princess Caroline of Monaco.

Carolyn a form of Carolina.

Carrie a form of Carol. Carrie Bradshaw, fictional heroine of *Sex and the City*. **Kaari.**

Carrie Ann a combination of Carrie and Ann.

Carson Scottish: transferred use of a surname.

Carter English: transferred use of a surname which refers to someone who used a cart to carry things.

Carys Welsh: loved one. **Karis**.

Casey Irish: brave one. **Kace**.

Cassandra Greek: she who enmeshes others; one who inspires people to yearn with love. **Cassondra, Sandy, Cass, Cassie, Casey**.

Cassidy Irish: curly-haired one.

Cassie a short form of Cassandra.

Caterina Portuguese: a form of Catherine.

Catharine a form of Catherine.

Catherine Greek: pure. **Catharine, Cathy, Cat, Caterina, Cathina, Cathleen, Caitlin, Catriona, Kit, Kitty**.

Cathina Italian: a form of Catherine.

Cathleen Irish: a form of Catherine.

Catriona Welsh: a form of Catherine.

Cayenne Tupi Indian: the dried ground-up form of a hot pepper.

Cécile French: a form of Cecilia.

Cecilia Latin: melodious; one with gray-colored eyes. **Cécile, Celia, Cecily, Cicely, Cissy, Silja**.

Cecily a form of Cecilia.

Celeste French: heavenly one. Celeste Holm, American actress. **Celesta, Celestine**.

Céline a form of Selena.

Cecily a form of Cecilia.

Celia Latin: celestial.

Cerise French: cherry.

Chandler English: transferred use of a surname that refers to someone who made and sold candles.

Chanel Old French: one who lives near the canal, or channel; also, transferred use of a surname. Coco Chanel, the French perfume maker and iconic fashion designer.

Channing English: wise one.

Chantal French: a place name in France meaning stone, but also, a surname, most famously that of a 17th-century woman who founded an order of nuns. **Chantel, Shantae, Shantay.**

Chapin English: transferred use of a surname.

Charis Greek: full of grace.

Charise Greek: grace; a reference to the three Graces in classical mythology. **Sharise.**

Charity Latin: devoted; munificent; altruistic. **Charita, Cherry.**

Charla a form of Charlotte.

Charlene a form of Charlotte.

Charlie a form of Charlotte.

Charlize a form of Charlotte. Charlize Theron, American actress.

Charlotte Saxon: a robust and dignified woman; a feminine form of Charles. **Charlene, Charla, Charlie, Charlize, Carlotta, Letty, Lottie, Lotta, Tetty, Tottie.**

Charmaine Latin: a short song of happiness.

Chase English: transferred use of a surname referring to someone who hunts or gives chase.

Chelsea English: a ship's port. **Kelsey.**

Cher French: dear and beloved. Cher, stage name of an American actress.

Cheri French: one who is adored; a darling. **Cherie, Chérie, Sherri, Cheryl.**

Cherilyn a form of Cheryl and Lynn.

Cherish English: to adore; to feel much affection for.

Cherry English: a version of the French word chérie, which is a term of endearment meaning loved one; also, a stone fruit.

Cheryl a form of Cheri. Cheryl Tiegs, American actress. **Sheryl, Sherilyn, Cherilyn.**

Cheyenne Native American: tribe from the western plains; a city in Wyoming named for this tribe.

Chiara Italian: a form of Clara.

China English: a huge country in East Asia; also, a delicate pottery.

Chloe Greek: new blossoms; lush; young grass. Chloe Sevigny, American actress.

Christa German: a form of Christine.

Christelle French: a form of Christine.

Christiane French: a form of Christine.

Christina Greek: a form of Christine. **Crystal, Cristina, Tina.**

Christine Greek: Christ's holy breath; also, Latin: a follower of Christ; a feminine of Christian. **Cristine, Chris, Chrissie, Chrissy, Christy. Kirstie, Kirstin, Kristin, Christa, Christina, Christelle, Christiane, Teena.**

Christmas Old English: a holiday observed by Christians celebrating the birth of Christ, the Christian prophet.

Christy a pet form of Christine. **Chrissy, Chrissie.**

Chrysanthe Greek: an ornamental flower also, used for medicine and as a pesticide. **Chrysanthemum.**

Chudney English: transferred use of a surname.

Cian Irish: from a long line.

Ciara Irish: black-haired one. **Sierra.**

Cicely a form of Cecilia. Cicely Tyson, American actress.

Cindy a form of Cynthia. Cindy Crawford, American model.

Cinnamon Hebrew: the bark of a laurel tree prized for its culinary and medicinal uses; a fiery, aromatic spice; also, refers to a reddish color.

Cissy English: a form of Sissy, Sister, and Cecilia. Sister Parish, pet name of American interior designer.

Claire a form of Clara. Clare Booth Luce, American diplomat and author. **Clare.**

Clara Latin: sunny; brilliant; shining or memorable. **Claire, Clare, Clarice, Chiara.**

Clarice Italian: a form of Clara.

Clarissa Latin: the most brilliant or most beautiful; a person who is destined to be famous. **Clarice**.

Claudette French: a form of Claudia. Claudette Colbert, French-born actress.

Claudia Latin: one who walks with a limp; feminine form of Claudius. **Claude, Claudie, Claudine, Claudette**.

Claudie a form of Claudia. **Claude**.

Clea Greek: a form of Cleopatra.

Clémance French: to give leniency or mercy.

Clementine Latin: sympathetic, tender, forgiving; a feminine form of Clement.

Cleo a short form of Cleopatra. **Cleona**.

Cleopatra Greek: the grandeur of a famous father. **Cleo, Clea**.

Cloris Greek: blooming flowers; also, a Greek goddess. **Chloris**.

Clothilde Saxon: a maiden of an illustrious battle. **Clotilda**.

Clover English: a green flower used to enrich the earth for planting crops. **Clove, Clovis**.

Clytie Greek: splendid one. A mythological woman, who died of unrequited love and became the heliotrope plant, whose face (a flower) always turns to the sun.

Coco Spanish: the coconut palm or its fruit. Nickname of Chanel.

Colleen Irish: a lassie. Colleen Dewhurst, Canadian-born actress.

Collete Latin: triumphant one. Colette Sidonie-Gabrielle, French author. **Colletta**.

Columba Italian: dove.

Concetta a form of Constance.

Connie a form of Constance. Connie Francis, American singer.

Constance Latin: rigid and obstinate; steadfast; trustworthy. Constance Bennett, American actress. **Con, Connie, Concetta, Constantine**.

Cookie Dutch: a diminutive of the word "cake;" this is a common pet name and can refer to a tough character, a good-looking woman, or a sweet girl.

Cora Greek: a young girl. **Coralie**, **Coretta**, **Corinna**, **Corinne**, **Corey**.

Coral English: a deep pink color; the rock-like skeletal deposit where colonies of tiny animals live in warm seas.

Coralena a form of Cora and Lena.

Coralie a combination of Coral and Lee. **Coralee**.

Coralyn a combination of Coral and Lynn.

Corbin Latin: a raven.

Cordelia Celtic: daughter of the ocean. Shakespeare's Cordelia, daughter of King Lear.

Corinna a form of Cora.

Cornelia Latin: integrity; like a woman; noble; feminine form of Cornelius. **Nell**, **Nellie**.

Corrine a form of Cora. **Corine**.

Cory Anne a combination of Cory and Anne.

Cosette French: a victorious people; also, a feminine form of Nicholas. Cosette, character in Victor Hugo's *Les Miserables*.

Cosima Italian: a feminine form of Cosmo; divine order; beauty.

Courtney Norman: transferred use of a surname of a place in northern France where the Normans were based and from which they went out to conquer other lands. Courteney Cox Arquette, American actress. **Courteney**.

Cricket English: a small insect characterized by the noise it makes when it rubs its feet together; also, a game popular in England; a term of endearment.

Cristina a form of Christina.

Crystal a form of Christina.

Cuddles English: to lie close together for warmth or affection; a term of endearment.

Cybille a form of Sibyl. Cybill Shepherd, American actress. **Cybill**, **Cybil**, **Sibyl**.

Cynthia Greek: the moon goddess. **Cindy**, **Cinder**.

Cypress Greek: an evergreen tree.

Cyprian Greek: one from Cyprus.

Daffodil English: a perennial bulbous herb with a large flower.

Dagmar Danish: happiness of the country. **Dag**.

Dahlia Old Norse: one from the valley; also, Scandinavian: a bright flower named after the Swedish botanist Anders Dahl.

Daisy Anglo-Saxon: a bright and large flower; the night following the day; happy; jolly.

Dakota Native American: tribe of northern Mississippi; also, two American states named after this tribe.

Dale Teutonic: one who lives in a valley. Dale Evans, American movie cowgirl. **Daile**.

Damaris Greek: a tree.

Damona a feminine form of Damon.

Dana Irish: from Denmark; the mythological mother of the gods. **Danae**.

Danica Slavic: a morning star.

Danielle French: a feminine form of Daniel, meaning God is my judge; in the Old Testament, Daniel was a prophet who was thrown into the lion's den and saved by divine province. Danielle Steel, American author. **Danny, Dany, Danya.**

Danya Hebrew: a feminine form of Daniel.

Daphne Greek: shy maiden of the laurel tree. **Daffy.**

Dara Hebrew: the heart of wisdom.

Darby English: transferred use of a surname referring to someone from Derby, which means deer settlement in Old Norse.

Darcy English: transferred use of a surname of Norman origin; usually referring to an aristocrat or upper-class person.

Daria Greek: a saint who was married to an Egyptian Christian and martyred in Rome. **Darina.**

Darina Czech: a form of Daria.

Darla a form of Darlene. Darla, little girl on *The Little Rascals*. **Darly, Darley.**

Darlene Anglo-Saxon: sweetheart; fondly and warmly loved. **Daryl, Darla, Darley, Darly.**

Darley a form of Darla. **Darly.**

Daryl a form of Darlene. Daryl Hannah, American actress.

Dawn Anglo-Saxon: the daybreak.

Deanna Latin: brilliant as the day. Deanna Durbin, Canadian-born actress and singer.

Deborah Hebrew: beelike; hard-working. Debbie Reynolds, American actress. **Debra, Debbie, Debby, Deb, Binky.**

Deidre Irish: sad one. **Didi, Dee, Deirdre.**

Delaney Irish: a child of the challenger. **Delayne, Lainey.**

Delia a form of Delilah.

Delicia Latin: delight; tasty.

Delilah Hebrew: one who entices. **Delia, Lila, Lilah, Lylie.**

Della Teutonic: a royal person. **Ella, Del**.

Delphine Greek: peace; tranquility. Delphina.

Demi Greek: a suffix meaning half. Demi Moore, American actress.

Denise Greek: wine goddess; a feminine form of Dennis.

Derry English: a form of Derek and Terry.

Desirée French: yearning; deliverance.

Destiny French: a preordained course of events; fate.

Devon English: the name of a city in southwest England.

Diamond Greek: the hardest mineral known on earth; a beautiful, brilliant, and very valuable crystal stone.

Diana Latin: virgin goddess of the moon. Diana, Princess of Wales. **Deanna, Deedee, Diane, Di, Diandra, Kiana**.

Diandra a form of Diana.

Diane a form of Diana.

Diantha Greek: a heavenly flower; in mythology, the flower of Zeus, the supreme god.

Dina English: a form of Dinah or Dino. **Dena, Didina**.

Dinah Hebrew: to take vengeance. **Dina, Dena, Didina**.

Dione Greek: the female child of heaven and earth. **Dionne**.

Dior French: golden one.

Dixie American: a girl from the American South. **Dix.**

Dodie a form of Doris. **Dody.**

Dolly a form of Dorothy. Dolly Parton, American country singer. **Dollie.**

Dominique French and Spanish: belonging to God; a feminine form of Dominic. **Dominica.**

Donna Italian: a lady. Donna Dixon, American actress.

Dora Greek: a present.

Doreen French: golden lass. **Dori, Dorene.**

Dori a form of Doreen.

Doria English: a form of Dorian.

Dorian Greek: the name of a place in Greece. **Doria.**

Doris Greek: goddess of the ocean. Doris Day, American actress. **Dodie, Dody.**

Dorothy Greek: a present from the divine; a feminine form of Theodore. Dorothy Parker, American writer. **Dora, Dollie, Dolly, Dorothée, Dorothea, Dot, Dottie.**

Drea a form of Andrea.

Dulcie Latin: charming; sweet. **Dulcy, Dulcine.**

Dustin English: transferred use of a surname which means stone of Thor.

Dusty English: a form of Dustin. Dusty Springfield, British singer.

Eartha Anglo-Saxon: the earth.

Ebony Egyptian: a beautiful, dark, black wood.

Echo Greek: a repeated sound; from the Greek myth of Narcissus and Echo.

Eda Anglo-Saxon: merry; rich. **Edda, Edie.**

Eden Hebrew: lovely; enchanting; epitomizing feminine characteristics.

Edie a short form of Edith. Edie Sedgwick, '60s model and film star.

Edina Teutonic: riches; amity; mirth. **Edna.**

Edith Teutonic: an expensive present; grand; noble; also, Saxon: the woman of high birth. Edith Wharton, American author. **Dita, Edie, Ediva.**

Edwina Anglo-Saxon: an affluent and treasured friend; a feminine form of Edwin. **Edina, Eddie, Winnie, Win.**

Effie Greek: well-regarded; beautiful; celebrated. **Eppie, Euphemia, Phemie.**

Egan Irish: the Celtic sun deity.

Eileen Greek: illumination; an Irish form of Helen. **Aileen, Aveline.**

Eilish Irish: a form of Elizabeth. **Eilis**.

Elaine Greek: brilliance; a French form of Helen. Elaine May, American comedian. **Alayne, Lane, Lainie, Lanie, Lani, Layne, Layna, Elena, Leanne**.

Elana a form of Alana.

Eleanor Greek: luminosity. **Eleanore, Eleanora, Elinor, Ella, Elle, Ellen, Ellie, Leonore, Nora**.

Electra Greek: radiant; a glowing star. **Elettra**.

Elena Greek: radiance. **Alayna**.

Eleni Greek: a form of Helen.

Elisa Saxon: faithful; dignified. **Elissa**.

Elise Hebrew: God's promise.

Elisha a form of Alisha.

Elissa a form of Elisa.

Elita Latin: chosen one. **Lita, Lida**.

Eliza a form of Elizabeth. **Lizzie**.

Elizabeth Hebrew: devoted to God; cordial; motivated. Elizabeth Taylor, British-born actress. **Liz, Lizzie, Lisbette, Lisbeth, Eliza, Elisabetta, Elsbeth, Elspeth, Eilish, Eilis, Beth, Bethia, Bette, Betty, Bettiann, Betsy, Bets, Bess, Bessie, Bettina, Liesl**.

Ella English: a short form of many names, including Eleanor and Ellen. Ella Fitzgerald, American singer.

Elle French: a pronoun used to refer to a female. Elle MacPherson, Australian model.

Ellen Greek: luminosity. **Ella, Ellie, Ennie**.

Ellie a form of Ellen.

Elliot English: transferred use of a surname; a form of Ellis.

Ellis English: transferred use of a surname, referring to the Old Testament prophet Elijah. **Elliot**.

Élodie French: foreign wealth; also, a form of Melody. **Elodie**.

Eloise Teutonic: legendary in battle. Kay Thompson and Hilary Knight's Eloise, fictional young resident of the Plaza Hotel. **Heloise, Louisa, Louise**.

Elsa Teutonic: of royal birth; also, French: wistful; quixotic. Elsa Schiaparelli, Italian-born fashion designer. **Ilsa, Elsie.**

Elsbeth a form of Elizabeth.

Elsie a form of Elsa.

Elspeth a form of Elizabeth.

Elvie a form of Elvira.

Elvira Latin: just; open-minded; also, Teutonic: elfin. **Elvie.**

Elysia Greek: celestial joy. **Elise, Ilsa.**

Emanuelle Hebrew and French: God is among us; the name of the Messiah pledged by God.

Emeline Teutonic: hard-working; academic. **Emiline, Emelina, Emmy.**

Emerald Old French: a beautiful green gem. **Esmerelda.**

Emerson American: transferred use of a surname. Ralph Waldo Emerson, poet.

Emily Latin: one who compliments; also, Teutonic: diligent; inventive. **Amelia, Emilie, Amalie, Emmie, Emme, Amelinda.**

Emlyn Teutonic: hard-working; also, Welsh: devotee.

Emma Teutonic: one who nurses to health; ancestor; collective; full of life. Emma Thompson, British actress. **Em.**

Emma Rae a combination of Emma and Rae.

Emme a form of Emily. **Emmy.**

Ena Irish: passionate.

Enid Celtic: wholesome; honorable; a woodlark.

Ennie a form of Ellen.

Eppie a form of Effie.

Erica Teutonic: always fierce; forever noble; a feminine form of Eric. **Rickie, Rika, Rikki.**

Erin Irish: serene; calm. **Erina.**

Esmé French and Anglo-Saxon: compassionate guardian. **Esme, Esmée.**

Esmeralda Greek: a beautiful green jewel; brilliant optimism. **Esmerelda.**

Essie a form of Esther.

Estee a form of Esther.

Estelle Latin: a star. **Estella, Stella, Estrella, Estrellita.**

Esther Hebrew: a star; lucky. **Easter, Essa, Esta, Estee, Essie, Hester, Hettie, Istar, Stella.**

Ethel Teutonic: royal; leader. Lucy's best friend on *I Love Lucy*, Ethel Mertz, played by American actress, Vivian Vance. **Ethelin, Ethyl.**

Etoile French: fate; destiny; following one's star.

Etta Teutonic: little; one who rules the home or homeland. **Ettie.**

Ettie a form of Etta.

Eudora Greek: munificent; a happy present. Eudora Welty, American author. **Dora.**

Eugenia Greek: of royal birth; a feminine form of Eugene. Empress Eugenie, wife of Napoleon III. **Eugenie, Genya.**

Eulalia Greek: one who converses eloquently. **Lallie, Eula, Eulalie.**

Eustacia Greek: calm; steadfast; verdant. **Stacia, Stacey.**

Eva a form of Evangeline. **Ava.**

Evan Welsh: a form of John.

Evangeline Greek: one who carries happy tidings. **Eva, Ava.**

Eve Hebrew: animation; life. **Ebba, Evie, Evita, Evonne, Naeva.**

Evelia a form of Evelyn.

Evelyn Celtic: enjoyable; illumination; life. **Aveline, Evelynn, Evelien, Evelia, Evy, Linnie.**

Ever Old English: at any time at all.

Evette a form of Yvette. **Ivette.**

Evonne a form of Yvonne.

Evy a form of Evelyn.

f

Fabia Latin: one who grows beans; a feminine form of Fabian. **Fabiana, Fabienne.**

Fabiana Italian: a form of Fabia.

Fabienne French: a form of Fabia.

Fabrice French: one who knows and works a craft; one who makes things.

Faith Latin: loyal; credulous. **Fae, Fay, Faye, Faythe.**

Fancy Greek: caprice.

Fanny Teutonic: liberated. **Fannie.**

Fantasia Greek: the imagination. **Fantine.**

Fantine a form of Fantasia.

Farrell Irish: transferred use of a surname.

Fauve French: a wild animal; a school of painting characterized by the use of bright colors, lead by Henri Matisse, and followed by Paul Gauguin.

Fawn Latin: a baby deer. **Faunie.**

Fay French: an elfin creature. **Faye, Fayette, Fayme.**

Fayette French: a form of Fay.

Felice Latin: happy; ecstatic. **Felicity, Felicia.**

Felicia a form of Felice.

Felicity a form of Felice.

Fern Greek: a feather.

Fernanda Teutonic: one who lives life as an adventure; a feminine form of Ferdinand.

Fifi French: a familiar form of Josephine; also, Hebrew: one who will add. **Fifine.**

Finella Irish: a form of Finola. **Fenella.**

Finola Irish: one with white shoulders. **Finella, Fenella.**

Fiona Irish: fair-skinned. **Vionna.**

Flannery Irish: red-haired. Flannery O'Connor, American author.

Flavia Latin: blond.

Fletcher English: transferred use of a surname; referring to an arrow maker.

Fleur a form of Flora.

Flora Latin: a botanical flower. **Fleur, Fleurette, Flower.**

Florence Latin: blossoming; well-to-do. Florence Nightingale, nursing pioneer born in Florence Italy. **Fiorenza, Flo, Florrie, Flossy.**

Florrie a form of Florence.

Flossy a form of Florence.

Flower English: a form of Flora.

Flynn Irish: child of the red-haired man.

Forsythia New Latin: a flower olive shrub named for the botanist William Forsyth.

Fortune Latin: lucky. **Fortuna.**

Frances Latin: liberated; a feminine form of Francis. **Fanchette, Francine, Franny, Frankie, Francesca, François.**

Francesca Italian: a form of Frances.

Francine French: a form of Frances.

Françoise French: a form of Frances.

Franny a familiar form of Frances. **Fran.**

Frederica Teutonic: diplomatic leader; a feminine form of Frederick. **Fred, Farica, Frédérique, Freddie, Rica, Rickie.**

Freesia Latin: a fragrant African herb with bright flowers, named for the botanist F.H.T. **Freese.**

Freya Old Norse: royal. **Fraya, Freja.**

Gabrielle Hebrew and French: from God's might; a feminine form of Gabriel. Gabrielle Bonheur "Coco" Chanel, French fashion designer. **Gabby, Gavra.**

Gail Anglo-Saxon: glad; full of life. **Gayle, Gael, Gayla, Gayleen.**

Galena Greek: calm; a healer.

Galina Russian: a form of Helen.

Gardenia Latin: a white flower; also, Teutonic: from the garden.

Garland Latin: a necklace made of flowers.

Garnet Latin: a deep red, brilliant jewel.

Gay Teutonic: happy; carefree; dynamic. **Gaye.**

Gayden English: transferred use of a surname.

Gelsey English: jasmine. **Gelsy, Gelsi.**

Gemma Latin: a precious gem; valuable jewel. **Gem, Jemma.**

Geneva Old French: a juniper tree. **Gena, Janeva.**

Geneviéve Teutonic: white; light; unassuming; a white sea swell. **Gennie, Guinevere, Jenny.**

Georgette French: a form of Georgia.

Georgia Greek: one who loves the earth; female dignity; a feminine form of George. **Georgiana, Georgy, Geordie, Georgina, Georgette.**

Georgy a form of Georgia. **Geordie.**

Geraldine Teutonic: a fierce spear; a feminine form of Gerald. **Geri, Dina, Deena, Giralda, Jeralee.**

Geralyn a combination of Gerri and Lynn. **Gerilyn, Jerilyn.**

Germaine Latin: of German heritage. Germaine Greer, Australian-born feminist writer.

Gertie a form of Gertrude.

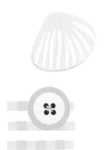

Gertrude Teutonic: all knowing; mighty spear. Gertrude Stein, American writer. **Gert, Gerta, Gerda, Trudy, Gertie.**

Ghislaine English: a form of Giselle.

Gia Italian: a feminine form of Gianni.

Giana Italian: a form of Giovanni and John. **Gianna, Gianina, Giovanna.**

Gidget a pet name.

Gigi French: a common pet name; a short form of Virginia and Georgia.

Gilberta Teutonic: brilliant potential; a feminine form of Gilbert. **Berta, Bertie, Gilbertina, Gill, Gilli.**

Gilda Celtic: the right hand of God; also, Anglo-Saxon: covered in gold. **Golda.**

Gillian a form of Jill. **Jillian.**

Gina Latin: a queen.

Ginger Latin: a spicy rhizome prized for its culinary and medicinal uses. Ginger Rogers, American dancer and actress.

Ginny English: a familiar form of Virginia.

Giovanna Italian: a form of Giana.

Gisela German and Dutch: a form of Giselle.

Giselle German: a promise; in medieval Europe, children were often given from one royal court to another as a show of alliance. *Giselle*, a romantic ballet. **Gisela, Ghislaine.**

Gladys Latin: delicate; modest; competent; gladiolus; a feminine form of Claude. **Gladie, Gladine.**

Glenda a form of Glenna.

Glenna Celtic: one who is from a secluded, narrow valley; a feminine form of Glenn. **Glen, Glenda, Glenna, Glennie, Glynnis.**

Glennie a familiar form of Glenna.

Gloria Latin: splendid. Gloria Steinem, American feminist. **Glorianna, Glory.**

Glynnis a form of Glenna. Glynis Johns, South African-born actress. **Glynis, Glenys.**

Golda Teutonic: blond. Goldie Hawn, American actress. **Goldie, Gilda, Goldarina.**

Grace Latin: elegant; striking; full of appreciation; God's blessing. **Engracia, Gracie, Gracia, Grazia, Gratiana.**

Grayson English: a feminine use of a boy's name, meaning bailiff's son.

Greer Greek: vigilant; a feminine form of Gregory.

Greta Greek: a pearl. Greta Garbo, Swedish-born actress. **Gretel, Gretl, Gretchen.**

Gretchen a form of Greta. Gretchen Mol, American actress.

Gretel a form of Greta. **Gretl.**

Guinevere Celtic: a white sea crest; fair-skinned. **Fredi, Gen, Gwenie, Winnie, Gwyn, Oona, Una, Winnie.**

Gwendolyn Celtic: academic; sympathetic. **Gwen, Wendy, Wynn, Windy, Winnie, Wendelin.**

Gwyneth Celtic: white; sacred. Gwyneth Paltrow, American actress. **Gwyn, Gwinnie, Winnie.**

h

Haden English: from the heather-covered hill. **Haiden**.

Haidee Greek: timid; honorable; selfless.

Haley Irish: scientific; brilliant. Haley Mills, British actress. **Hayley**.

Hallie Greek: enamored by the ocean; a feminine form of Henry and Harold. **Haley, Hailey, Hayley, Haleigh, Halimeda**.

Halsey English: from Hall's island.

Hana Japanese: a blossom. **Hanako**.

Hannah Hebrew: full of charity; generous; prayerful; good. **Anita, Anya, Ninetta**.

Happy English: blissful.

Harmony Latin: accord; concurrence.

Harper English: transferred use of a surname referring to someone who plays the harp. (Nelle) Harper Lee, American writer.

Harrah English: transferred use of a surname.

Harriet Teutonic: a lady of the home; head of the household; a feminine form of Henry. Harriet Beecher Stowe, American author. **Harri, Hattie**.

Harris English: transferred use of a surname.

Haru Japanese: spring.

Hattie a form of Harriet.

Haven Old English: a place of safety.

Hayley a form of Hallie.

Hazel Teutonic: a hazelnut tree; an order for action. **Aveline**.

Heather Anglo-Saxon: a small, purple, fragrant flower. **Heath**.

Heaven Old English: a spiritual place where people go after death to be with the deity; a place of beauty and light.

Hedda Teutonic: a clash; a loose, flowing garment. Hedda Hopper, American gossip columnist and actress. **Hedwig, Edvig, Hedy, Heddy**.

Hedley English: transferred use of a surname referring to a clearing in the heather field.

Helen Greek: light. This is probably the oldest feminine name in existence, and has many variations. Helen Keller, American author. **Ellen, Eleni, Helena, Helene, Hélène, Nell, Nora, Galina**.

Helena Greek: a form of Helen. **Yelena**.

Hélène French: a form of Helen. **Helene**.

Heloise Teutonic: splendid warrior. Heloise, French 12th-century woman, who corresponded with philosopher Peter Abelard.

Henna Arabic: a plant known for its reddish-brown dye.

Henrietta Teutonic: one who rules the home; royal lady; feminine form of Henry. **Henriette, Netty, Yetta, Enrichetta, Etta**.

Hermione Greek: of the earth; a feminine form of Herman. Hermione Baddeley, British actress. **Erma, Hermia, Ione**.

Hester Persian: star; good luck. Hester Prynne, heroine of Nathaniel Hawthorne's *The Scarlet Letter*. **Esther, Hesper, Hettie, Hetty, Heddy**.

Hettie German: a form of Hester. **Hetty, Heddy**.

Hilaire French: a form of Hilary.

Hilary Latin: jolly. **Hillary, Hilaire**.

Hinda Yiddish: a deer.

Holland Dutch: a European country, also, called The Netherlands. Holland Taylor, American actress.

Hollis English: from the place near the holly bushes.

Holly Anglo-Saxon: the holly bush; good luck. Holly Hunter, American actress.

Honesty Latin: truth; integrity.

Honey Old English: sweet; one who is loved; a pet name between lovers.

Honor Latin: principled. Honor Fraser, Scottish model. **Honore, Honora, Annora**.

Hope Anglo-Saxon: confidence; aspiration; prospect; joyful; trust.

Hortense Latin: perfumed; sweet-scented; one who gardens.

Hoshi Japanese: star.

Hoshiko Japanese: little star.

Huette Teutonic: a little, quick girl.

Hunter Old English: one who pursues, mostly in reference to killing animals for food.

Hyacinth Greek: a purple flower. **Cynthia, Jacinta, Jacks**.

i

Ianthe Greek: a purple flower; wonderful.

Ida Teutonic: hard-working; full of youth and vigor; rich; happy. **Idette, Idelle.**

Ileana Greek: one who is from Ilium or Troy. **Ilyana.**

Ilka Slavic: hard-working; full of life; one who flatters.

Ilona Hungarian: gorgeous; striking. **Ilonka.**

Ilsa Hebrew: God's promise. **Elsa.**

Iman Arabic: faith in God. **Imani.**

Imani Arabic: a form of Iman.

Imelda Spanish: the whole battle.

Imogen Latin: a picture; image; sympathy for all who are in need.

Ina Greek: wholesome; unadulterated.

India English: a subcontinent in Southeast Asia.

Indigo Greek: a deep blue color or the dye obtained from an indigo plant.

Inés Spanish: wholesome; unadulterated; tender; modest. **Inez.**

Inga Old Norse: female child; young leader in battle.

Ingrid Old Norse: splendid; female child of a war hero. Ingrid Bergman, Swedish-born actress.

Inka Polish and Russian: heavenly one.

Iola Greek: a clouded daybreak; a purple color. **Iole**.

Iolanthe a form of Yolanda. Iolanthe, Gilbert and Sullivan fairy.

Ione Greek: a valuable purple gemstone. Ione Skye, British-born actress. **Iona**.

Iphigenia Greek: sacrificed one. **Iphigenie**.

Ireland Irish: a small island to the west of England.

Irene Greek: calm; peace. **Irena**, **Rena**.

Iris Greek: the rainbow; a showy flower; the color in an eye.

Isa Teutonic: very strong-willed; determined. **Isabella**.

Isabel Hebrew: promised to God. **Isabelle**, **Isabella**, **Belle**, **Izzy**.

Isabella a form of Isabel. Isabella Rossellini, Italian-born actress.

Isadora Greek: a present from Isis, the Egyptian goddess of the moon. **Dora**, **Dory**.

Isolde Irish: light; beautiful; also, Old German: a fair maiden. Isolde, medieval lover of Tristram. **Isolda**, **Isola**.

Iva Hebrew: a bountiful offering from God; also, French: a yew tree.

Ivette a form of Yvette. **Evette**.

Ivora Scandinavian: a feminine form of Ivor, which refers to a bow and the military.

Ivory Egyptian: the white tusk of an animal, usually an elephant; white.

Ivy Hebrew: a climbing vine.

Izzy a form of Isabel.

j

Jacey American: from the letters "J" and "C."

Jacinda Greek: a purple flower; the hyacinth; gorgeous.

Jacqueline Hebrew: one who unseats another; a feminine form of Jacob and Jacques. Jacqueline Kennedy Onassis, American first lady. **Jackie, Jacklyn, Jacqui, Jacks.**

Jada Spanish: a form of Jade.

Jade Spanish: a green stone. **Jada.**

James Hebrew: a name held by two disciples of Christ. **Jamie.**

Jameson a feminine form of James. **Jamison.**

Jan Scandinavian and Czech: a form of John.

Jane Hebrew: a generous offering from God. Jane Eyre, Charlotte Brontë's fictional heroine. **Janey, Janie, Janet, Janette, Jean, Jenine, Jeanette, Shana, Siobhan.**

Janet Scottish: a form of Jane. **Janette.**

Janice Hebrew: God, who is gracious.

Jasmine Persian: a perfumed flower used for scents and for cuisine. **Jasmin, Yasmin, Jessamyn,**

Jessamine.

Jean Scottish: a form of Jane.

Jeanette a form of Jane. Jeanette MacDonald, American singer and actress.

Jemima Arabic: tranquility; wholesome; a dove. **Mimi**.

Jena a form of Jennifer. **Jenna**.

Jenine a form of Jane. **Jeanine**.

Jennifer Celtic: light-skinned; lovely of face. **Jen, Jenny, Jena**.

Jessamyn French: a form of Jasmine. **Jessamine**.

Jessica Hebrew: God's bounty; riches. **Jessie, Jess, Jessa**.

Jewel Latin: a precious gemstone; wonderful. Jewel, American singer. **Jewell**.

Jill Greek: a young person; also, Old English: a darling girl. Jill Clayburgh, American actress. **Jilly, Jillian, Gillian**.

Jillian a form of Jill.

Joan Hebrew: God's generous gift. Joni, Joanie, Joanna, Johanna, Joanne.

Joanna a form of Joan. **Johanna, Joanne**.

Joanne a form of Joanna.

Jocasta English: Oedipus's mother (and also, his wife) in classical legends.

Jocelyn Latin: happy; judicious; open-minded. **Joselyn**.

Jodie Hebrew: praised one; also, English: a pet form of Judith or Joe. **Jody**.

Joe Hebrew: one who increases; a pet name for girl's names that start with "Jo." **Joey, Jodie**.

Joelle French: a feminine form of Joel, which is a Hebrew name meaning "God."

Joey a form of Joe.

Johanna a form of Joanna.

Joie French: a form of Joy.

Jolie French: pretty; pleasant. **Jolly**.

Jolly English: a form of Jolie.

Joni a form of Joan. **Joanie**.

Jonna a feminine form of John.

Johnna, Jonnie.

Jonquil English: a flower similar to a daffodil.

Jordan English: a child baptized in water from the River Jordan. **Jordana, Jordanna**.

Jordana a form of Jordan. **Jordanna**.

Josephina a form of Josephine.

Josephine Hebrew: a remuneration. **Josephina, Josette, Josie**.

Josette a form of Josephine.

Josie a form of Josephine.

Joy Latin: delight; mirth. **Joya, Joie**.

Joyce Latin: rejoicing.

Juana Spanish: a feminine form of John.

Jude a form of Judith.

Judi a form of Judith.

Judith Hebrew: one who is loved and worshipped. **Judy, Judi, Jude, Jodie**.

Judy a form of Judith.

Jules a form of Julia.

Julia Latin: unpredictable; changeable; youthful; a feminine form of Julius. **Jules, Julie, Jewell, Julianne, Juliana**.

Juliana a form of Julia.

Julianne a form of Julia.

Julie a form of Julia.

Juliet Latin: a Roman clan name meaning downy. Juliet Capulet, from Shakespeare's *Romeo and Juliet*. **Juliette**.

June Latin: a child born in the month of June; youthful. **Junie**.

Justina a form of Justine.

Justine Latin: the honorable; a feminine form of Justin. **Justina**.

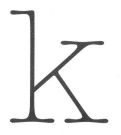

Kaari a form of Carrie.

Kace a form of Casey.

Kady a form of Katie.

Kaitlyn a form of Katherine and Lynn.

Kali Sanskrit: full of dynamic energy.

Kara Greek: wholesome and unadulterated.

Karen Greek: wholesome; lovely; very smart. **Karin**, **Caron**, **Karenna**, **Karina**.

Karenna a form of Karen.

Karina a form of Karen.

Karis Greek: graceful one. **Carys**.

Karla Teutonic: mighty; a feminine form of Charles. **Carly**.

Karsten Greek: anointed one.

Kate a form of Katherine. **Katie**.

Katharine a form of Katherine. Katharine Hepburn, American actress.

Katherine Greek: wholesome; virtuous. **Katharine, Catherine, Catharine, Kate, Katie, Kath, Kathy, Cathy, Kathleen, Kathlyn, Katinka, Katrina, Katya, Kit, Kitty, Carina, Kaitlyn, Caitlin.**

Kathleen Greek: a form of Katherine.

Kathlyn a form of Katherine.

Katie a form of Katherine. **Kady, Cady.**

Katinka a form of Katherine.

Katrina a form of Katherine.

Katya a form of Katherine. **Katia.**

Kay Greek: celebrating good fortune. **Kayla, Kaylee, Kaylyn, Keylyn.**

Kayla a form of Kay.

Kayley Irish: transferred use of a surname. **Kaylee.**

Kaylyn a form of Kay.

Keaton English: transferred use of a surname.

Keddy Scottish: a form of Adam, occasionally used for girls.

Keegan Irish: transferred use of a surname.

Keelin Irish: slim; white. **Keelyn.**

Keely Irish: lovely; splendid. **Keelyn.**

Keenan Irish: a form of Keene.

Keiko Japanese: honored.

Keisha African: a form of Keshia.

Kelly Irish: courageous; a young female warrior.

Kelsey a form of Chelsea. **Kelsy.**

Kendall Welsh: transferred use of a surname; refers to the season of spring. **Kenna.**

Kendra English: a feminine form of Kendrick; a high hill.

Kenna a form of Kendall.

Kennedy Irish: transferred use of a surname that originally meant "ugly head."

Kenyon Irish: blond one.

Kenzie a form of Mackenzie.

Kerry Irish: a dark-complexioned person; one with dark hair.

Keshia African: the favorite one. **Keisha.**

Keylyn a form of Kay.

Kezia Hebrew: a cassia plant, known for its cinnamon bark. **Keziah, Ketzia.**

Kiah Irish: a form of Kiana.

Kiana Irish: ancient one; also, Hawaiian: a form of Diana; goddess. **Kia, Kiah, Kiann, Kianne.**

Kiara Irish: little dark one.

Kiki Spanish: pet name for names ending in "queta."

Kim Old English: splendid leader; royalty.

Kimba Old English: from the meadow by the royal fortress.

Kimball English: chief warrior.

Kimberly Hebrew: from the field before the royal stronghold or castle. **Kim, Kimi.**

Kimberlyn a combination of Kimberly and Lynn.

Kimi a form of Kimberly.

Kinga German: a form of Kunigunde, which means courageous in hard times.

Kioko Japanese: a happy child.

Kira Old Persian: sun. **Kyra.**

Kirby Old English: from the town with a church.

Kirstie a form of Christine. Kirstie Alley, American actress.

Kirstin a form of Christine.

Kisa Russian: a kitten.

Kisi Japanese: a long and happy life.

Kissa African: a baby born after twins.

Kit English: a form of Katherine; also, a young cat. **Kitty.**

Kitty a form of Katherine. Kitty Carlisle Hart, American actress.

Koffi African: born on a Friday.

Koko Japanese: a stork.

Kristin a form of Christine.

Kylie Irish: lovely; very smart. **Kyle.**

Kyoko Japanese: mirror.

Lacey Greek: merry. **Lacy**, **Laci**.

Lady Old English: a female, often used as a term of courtesy.

Laetitia Latin: happiness. **Tish**.

Lainie a form of Elaine. Lainie Kazan, American actress. **Lanie**, **Lani**.

Lala Slavic: tulip.

Lana Greek: illumination. Lana Turner, American actress. **Lanna**, **Lanny**.

Lane a form of Lanette.

Lanette Anglo-Saxon: a lane. **Lane**.

Lani Hawaiian: sky.

Lara Latin: illustrious. Lara, character in *Doctor Zhivago*, by Boris Pasternak.

Larissa Greek: jolly.

Lark Middle English: skylark; to sing; a prank.

Lassie Scottish: a young girl. Lassie, adorable and helpful television collie. **Lass**.

Laura Greek: the laurel; victory; fame. Laura Dern, American actress. **Laurie**, **Lori**, **Lauren**, **Laurel**, **Laurette**, **Lolly**, **Loring**.

Laurel Latin: glory; an emblem of distinction; a feminine form of Lawrence. Laurel Ulrich, American writer.

Lauren a form of Laura.

Laurette a form of Laura. Laurette Taylor, American actress.

Laurie a form of Laura.

Lavender Old French: a sweet-smelling purple herb.

Laverna Old French: coming from the season of spring. **Verna**, **Vern**, **Laverne**.

Lavinia Latin: cleansed; a lady from Rome. **Vin**.

Lavonne a form of Yvonne.

Layla a form of Leila.

Layna a form of Elaine.

Leah Hebrew: weary. **Liah**, **Lia**, **Lee**.

Leanne a form of Elaine.

Leatrice combination of Leah and Beatrice. Leatrice Joy, American silent film actress.

Leda Greek: a woman of distinction.

Lee Anglo-Saxon: grassland; pasture; also, Irish: poetic. Lee Remick, American actress. **Leigh**, **Leelee**, **Leah**, **Lia**, **Leann**.

Leigh a form of Lee.

Leila Persian: a pearl; also, Arabic: as dark as night. Leila Josefowicz, Canadian violinist. **Leyla**, **Layla**.

Leilani Hawaiian: celestial blossom.

Lena Greek: luminosity. Lena Horne, American singer.

Lenore Greek: brightness.

Leona Latin: lion; a feminine form of Leo. **Leonie**, **Leontyne**.

Leora Hebrew: light. **Liora**.

Lesley Celtic: one who is from a gray garrison. Lesley Gore, American singer. **Leslie**.

Leta Latin: elation.

Letitia Latin: happiness; glee; cheerfulness. Letitia Tyler, 19th-century American first lady. **Leticia**, **Tisha**, **Letty**, **Lettie**.

Letty a form of Letitia. **Lettie**.

Lexi a form of Alexandra.

Leyla a form of Leila.

Lia a form of Lee.

Liana Latin: a creeping plant that scales structures; a strong connection.

Libby Hebrew: dedicated to God.

Liberty Latin: autonomy; the power to do as one pleases.

Liesl a form of Elizabeth.

Lila a form of Delilah. **Lilah.**

Lilac Persian: the flower of the same name; a blue color.

Lilah a form of Delilah. **Lila.**

Lilianna a form of Lillian. **Lilijana, Ljiljana.**

Lilias a form of Lillian.

Lilith Arabic: one who belongs in the night.

Lillian Greek: lily flower; purity. Lillian Hellman, American playwright. **Lily, Lilly, Lilianna, Ljilijana, Lilias.**

Lily a form of Lillian. Lily Tomlin, American comedian and actress. **Lilly.**

Lilybelle Latin: a striking lily flower.

Lina Latin: enthralling.

Linda Latin: attractive. Linda Ronstadt, American singer. **Amelinda, Lyndie**

Lindsey Old English: one who is from an isle of ponds and linden trees; a feminine form of Lindsay. Lindsay Lohan, American actress. **Lindsay.**

Linette Celtic: graceful; also, Old French: little lioness. **Lynn, Linnie.**

Ling Chinese: dainty.

Linnea Old Norse: a tree that bears limes.

Linney a form of Lynn.

Linnie a form of Lynn.

Lisa Hebrew: a promise of God; Leonardo da Vinci's Mona Lisa; Lisa Loopner, Gilda Radner's *Saturday Night Live* character; Lisa Birnbach, American author. **Leesa, Lissa, Lissie, Liza, Lizzie, Lisette, Liza.**

Lisbeth Hebrew: consecrated to God.

Lisette French: a form of Lisa. Lisette Model, Austrian photographer.

Lissa a form of Lisa.

Lissie a form of Lisa.

Livia Latin: the olive. **Livvie**.

Liza a form of Elizabeth. Liza Minnelli, American singer and actress.

Logan Scottish: transferred use of a surname.

Lois Greek: battle maiden; brave; a beautiful vision; a feminine form of Lewis. Lois Lane, Superman's lady friend.

Lola Latin: melancholy; anguish; also, Teutonic: strong; a feminine form of Charles. **Lolita**.

Lolita a form of Lola. Vladimir Nabokov's Lolita.

Lolly a form of Laura.

London English: a city and port in England, the capital of the United Kingdom.

Lorelei Teutonic: a person who allures with song; fascinating. **Lurlene**.

Loretta a feminine form of Lawrence. Loretta Young, stage name of American actress.

Lori a form of Laura and Lorraine.

Loring a form of Laura.

Lorna Latin: the laurel; triumph; a feminine form of Lawrence. Lorna Luft, America singer. **Lorena, Lorning**.

Lorning a form of Lorna.

Lorraine Teutonic: celebrated soldier. **Lori**.

Lottie a form of Charlotte. **Lotta**.

Louisa a feminine form of Louis. Louisa May Alcott, American author.

Louise Teutonic: woman who fought in military skirmishes; a lovely apparition; also, a feminine form of Louis. Louise Brooks, American actress. **Louisa, Lou**.

Love Old English: to be devoted to; robust; gentle; fondness. **Lovie, Lovey**.

Lovie a form of Love. **Lovey**.

Luce a form of Lucie.

Lucia a form of Lucie.

Luciana a form of Lucie and Anna.

Lucie Latin: radiance; one who brings light; one who is born at dawn; a feminine form of Lucius. Lucie Arnaz, American actress and singer. **Lucy, Luz, Lucia, Luce, Lucita.**

Lucienne a form of Lucie and Ann.

Lucille Latin: luminescence. Lucille Ball, American comedian. **Lucy, Lucie, Lucinda.**

Lucinda a form of Lucille. **Cindy, Lucky.**

Lucy a form of Lucie or Lucille. Lucy Maud Montgomery, Canadian author.

Ludie Teutonic: loved by the people, modest; comes from the ancient name, Ludmilla.

Ludmilla a form of Mila and Ludie.

Lula Latin: giving reparations; one who mollifies; also, Old English: illustrious elf. Louella Parsons, Hollywood gossip columnist. **Ella, Louella, Lou, Lulu.**

Lulie English: to soothe.

Lulu a form of Lula. Lulu, British pop singer.

Luna Latin: the moon; radiant.

Lunetta Italian: a small moon. **Lunette.**

Lurline Teutonic: tempting. **Lura, Lurette.**

Lydia Greek: a woman from Lydia; sophisticated. **Lydie.**

Lydie a form of Lydia.

Lylie a form of Delilah.

Lynette a form of Lynn.

Lynn Anglo-Saxon: a tumbling surge of water; falls. **Lynne, Lynnie, Lynette.**

Lyric Greek: suitable for singing with the lyre or for being set to music and sung; high-spirited; extravagantly emotional.

Lyris Greek: the lyre or harp; harmonious. **Lyra.**

Lysandra Greek: liberator of humanity. **Sandra.**

m

Mab Celtic: hilarity; bliss. Queen Mab, fairy in legends. **Maeve; Mavis.**

Mabel Latin: endearing; affable. Mabel Normand, American actress. **Mae, Maybelle.**

Macey a form of Miriam. **Macy.**

Mackenzie Scottish: child of a wise leader. **Kenzie, Makenna.**

Maddie a form of Madeleine. **Maddy.**

Madeleine Hebrew: a woman from Magdala; splendid; a mighty pillar. Madeleine Boullongne, 17th-century French painter; Madeline, Ludwig Bemelmans' fictional little French student. **Madeline, Maddie, Maddy, Matty.**

Madge Greek: a pearl. Madge Syers, British athlete.

Madison Native American: a common geographical name.

Maeve a form of Mab. Maeve Binchy, Irish author.

Maggie a form of Margaret. Fictional character in *Cat on a Hot Tin Roof*.

Magnolia New Latin: one of many American and Asian shrubs with evergreen or deciduous leaves and bright flowers in early spring.

Mahala Hebrew: kindheartedness. Mahalia Jackson, American gospel singer. **Mahalia**.

Maia Greek: motherly; nurse. **Maya**.

Maida Anglo-Saxon: a young woman. Maida Heatter, American cookbook author. **Maydee**.

Maire a form of Mary.

Mairead Scottish: a form of Mary.

Maisie Greek: a pearl. Fictional character in Henry James's *What Maisie Knew*.

Majorca Spanish: a Spanish island popular with tourists for its beaches and warm weather.

Makenna a form of Mackenzie.

Mala Latin: bad.

Malina Hebrew: ancient tower; glorious.

Mallory Norman: transferred use of a surname meaning an unfortunate person.

Malvina Irish: valiant; a feminine form of Melvin.

Mamie a form of Margaret. Mamie Doud Eisenhower, first lady.

Mandy a form of Amanda.

Manon French: a form of Marie.

Manuela Spanish: God is among us; a feminine form of Emanuel.

Mara Hebrew: bitter.

Marcella Latin: one who belongs to Mars; bellicose; a feminine form of Marc. **Marcela, Marcelle, Marcy**.

Marcia Latin: of Mars; soldier; a feminine form of Marc. **Marsha**.

Marcy a form of Marcella.

Mardi French: Tuesday. **Mardie, Marty**.

Mare a form of Mary. Mare Winningham, American actress.

Maren a form of Mary. **Marin**.

Maret a form of Miriam. **Marette**.

Margaret Greek: a pearl. Margaret Mitchell, American author. **Maggie, Meg, Meggie, Mamie, Peg, Peggy, Pegeen, Rita, Megan, Margo, Margot, Margaux, Marjorie, Margery, Margit, Marguerite, Mysie, Marka, Marketa**.

Margaux a form of Margaret. Margaux Hemingway, American actress.

Margery a form of Margaret. **Marjory**, **Margie**.

Margit a form of Margaret.

Margo a form of Margaret.

Margot a form of Margaret.

Marguerite French: a form of Margaret; a daisy. Marguerite Perey, French physicist. **Daisy**, **Maggie**, **Rita**.

Maria a form of Mary. Maria Mayer, German-born scientist. **Marika**, **Mariko**.

Mariah a form of Mary. Mariah Carey, American singer.

Marian English: poised. Marian Anderson, American singer; Marianne Moore, American poet. **Marianne**, **Mariana**.

Mariana a form of Marian.

Maribel French: the lovely Mary.

Marie a form of Mary. Marie Curie, French scientist. **Manon**.

Mariel a form of Mary. Mariel Hemingway, American actress.

Marietta Italian: a form of Marie. Marietta Peabody Tree, American socialite; Mariette Hartley, American actress. **Mariette**.

Marigold Anglo-Saxon: one who is reminiscent of the golden marigold flower.

Marika Slavic: a form of Maria.

Mariko Slavic: a form of Maria.

Marilee a form of Mary.

Marilyn a form of Mary. Marilyn Monroe, American actress.

Marin a form of Mary.

Marina Latin: one who is of the sea. **Marine**, **Marnie**, **Marni**.

Marinda a form of Miriam.

Marine a form of Marina.

Maris Latin: ocean star. **Marissa**.

Marisol Spanish: bright ocean.

Marissa a form of Maris.

Maritza a form of Mary.

Marjorie a form of Margaret. Marjorie Morningstar, fictional character by Herman Wouk.

Marka Czech: a form of Margaret.

Marketa Czech: a form of Margaret.

Markie a feminine form of Marc. Markie Post, American actress.

Marla a form of Marlene.

Marlene Hebrew: lofty; above all else. Marlene Dietrich, German actress. **Marla, Marley, Marly.**

Marley a form of Marlene. Marley Shelton, American actress. **Marly.**

Marlin English: a large marine fish.

Marlo a form of Mary. Marlo Thomas, American actress.

Marly a form of Marlene.

Marnie a form of Marina. Marni Nixon, singer. **Marni.**

Marsha a form of Marcia. Marsha Mason, American actress.

Marta a form of Martha.

Martha Aramaic: a woman of distinction; one who leads the affairs of the home. Martha Stewart, American lifestyle entrepreneur; Martha Dandridge Washington, 1st American first lady. **Marthe, Marta.**

Marthe a form of Martha.

Martie a form of Martina.

Martina Latin: bellicose; fierce; a feminine form of Martin. Martina Navratilova, Czechoslovakian-born, American tennis champion. **Martie, Marty, Martine, Tina.**

Martine a form of Martina.

Marty a form of Martina. **Martie.**

Marvel Latin: astonishing; a miracle. **Marvella.**

Mary Hebrew: bitter. Mary Cassatt, painter. **Mare, Marie, Maria, Maren, Marin, Marilyn, Maritza, Mariah, Mariel, Marielle, Maribell, Mariette, Marietta, Maren, Marilee, Maryse, Maire, Mairead, Molly, Polly.**

Maryelle a form of Mary and Elle.

Maryellen a form of Mary and Ellen.

Maryjane a form of Mary and Jane.

Marylea a form of Mary and Lee.

Maryrose a form of Mary and Rose.

Maryse a form of Mary.

Masako Japanese: sand. Crown Princess Masako of Japan. **Masago**.

Maslin French: masculine name, meaning young Thomas, which is becoming more commonly used for girls.

Mason English: transferred use of a surname meaning one who builds with stone.

Mateja Czech: a form of Matthew.

Matilda Teutonic: a powerful fighter. **Mathilde, Tilly, Tillie, Tilda, Maud, Maude, Maudie, Mattie.**

Mattie a form of Matilda.

Maud a form of Matilda. **Maude, Maudie.**

Maura a form of Maureen.

Maureen Irish: little Mary; also, Old French: one with dark skin. Maureen Stapleton, American actress. **Maura, Mo, Moira, Morena.**

Mauve Latin: a mild purple color.

Mavis Celtic: a songbird.

Maxie a form of Maxine.

Maxine Latin: the maximum; above all others; a feminine form of Maximilian. Maxene Andrews, American singer. **Max, Maxie, Maxime, Maxene.**

May Latin: born in May; great one; also, Anglo-Saxon: kinswoman; also, Middle English: maiden. **Mae.**

Maya a form of Maia.

Maydee a form of Maida.

Meadow Old English: pasture; grassland. Meadow Soprano, television mobster's daughter.

Meg a form of Margaret.

Megan Greek: resilient; stately.

Meka a form of Michelle and Michaela. **Mika**.

Mel a form of Melanie.

Melanie Greek: dark; under cover of night; clad in black. Melanie, American '60s singer. **Mel**.

Melina Greek: placid; also, Latin; the color of the yellow canary.

Melinda Greek: pliable; tenderhearted.

Melisande a form of Melissa.

Melissa Greek: sweet honey produced by a bee; a bee. Melissa Gilbert, American actress. **Melisande, Missy**.

Melody Greek: a harmony. **Melodie, Élodie, Elodie**.

Meraud Cornish: from the sea.

Mercedes Spanish: forgiving. Mercedes McCambridge, American actress. **Mercy**.

Mercy a form of Mercedes.

Meredith Old Welsh: wonderful; also, Celtic: protector from the ocean depths.

Merewen Irish: a feminine form of Marvin.

Merilee a form of Merry. **Merrily**.

Meritt Anglo-Saxon: of value.

Merle Latin: a blackbird. **Merlye**.

Merry Anglo-Saxon: amiable; joyful; ecstatic. **Merilee, Merrily**.

Meryl a form of Muriel. Meryl Streep, American actress.

Meta Latin: ambitious.

Mia Latin: mine; something that belongs to me. Mia Farrow, American actress.

Michael a form of Michelle. Michael Learned, American actress.

Michaela a form of Michelle. **Meka**.

Michaelyn a form of Michelle.

Micheline a form of Michelle.

Michelle Hebrew: Who is like God?; a feminine form of Michael. **Michele, Mitchie, Micheline, Michael, Michaela, Michaelyn, Meka, Mika, Mickey, Midge**.

Mickey a form of Michelle.

Midge a form of Michelle. The doll Barbie's best friend.

Midori Japanese: green. Midori, Japanese violinist.

Miette French: little, sweet.

Mignon Old French: refined; fragile; dear.

Mika a form of Michelle. **Meka**.

Mila Slavic: beloved; a form of the ancient name, Ludmilla. Milla Jovovich, Russian actress. **Milla, Mylie, Milea**.

Milagros Spanish: a miracle.

Mildred Teutonic: temperate advisor; easygoing authority. Mildred Pierce, fictional film character, played by Joan Crawford. **Millie, Milly**.

Millicent Teutonic: conscientious; robust. Millicent Rogers, art patron. **Millie, Milly**.

Millie a form of Mildred and Millicent. **Milly**.

Mimi a form of Miriam.

Mina a form of Wilhelmina.

Mindy Teutonic: adoration; tribute.

Minerva Greek: sagacity. **Minnie, Minna**.

Minette a form of Wilhelmina.

Minka a form of Wilhelmina.

Minna a form of Minerva.

Minnie a form of Minerva.

Minty a form of Araminta.

Mirabel Latin: exceedingly lovely; astounding. **Mirabelle, Belle**.

Miranda Latin: commendable. **Myra, Randy**.

Mireille French: miracle; a wonder.

Miriam Hebrew: pungent; defiant. **Macey, Macy, Marinda, Mitzi, Mimi**.

Missy a form of Melissa.

Misty Old English: covered in mist.

Mitzi a form of Miriam. Mitzi Gaynor, American actress.

Miyuki Japanese: deep snow; peaceful.

Moira Greek: praiseworthy; also, Celtic: gentle; also, Irish: exalted.

Molly a form of Mary. Molly Pitcher, American Revolution heroine. **Mollie**.

Mona Greek: on one's own; one of a kind; also, Celtic: exalted; gallant.

Monet French: descended from the protectors. Claude Monet, French painter.

Monica Greek: insight; success; also, Latin: counselor. **Monique**.

Monique a form of Monica.

Montana Latin: mountain; also, a state.

Morgan a form of Morgana. Morgan Llwyd, 17th-century Welsh writer.

Morgana Old Welsh: one is from the ocean's edge. **Morgan**.

Muffy American: term of endearment. **Muffie**.

Muriel Arabic: myrrh; pungent; also, Irish: luminescent ocean. **Meryl**.

Murphy Irish: warrior from the sea; transferred use of a surname. Murphy Brown, television reporter played by Candice Bergen.

Musetta a form of Musette.

Musette Old French: a hushed, gentle song. **Musetta**.

Mylea a feminine form of Milo. **Mylie**.

Mylie a form of Mila.

Myra Greek: copious; also, Latin: magnificent.

Myrna Irish: tender; gracious.

Myrtle Greek: myrtle; a crown bestowed for success.

Mysie a form of Margaret.

n

Nadia a form of Nadine. Nadia Comaneci, Romanian gymnast.

Nadine Slavic: expectation. Nadine Gordimer, South African author. **Nadia**.

Naeva French: a form of Eve.

Nan a form of Nancy.

Nancy Hebrew: poise. Nancy Drew, fictional girl sleuth by Carolyn Keene; Nancy Mitford, British author. **Nan, Nance, Nanny, Nanette**.

Nanette a form of Nancy.

Nanny a form of Nancy.

Naomi Hebrew: agreeable; charming. **Noemi**.

Narcissa a form of Narcisse.

Narcisse Greek: a daffodil. **Narcissa**.

Narda Persian: one who is anointed; perfumed; thrilled.

Natalia a form of Natalie.

Natalie Latin: natal or birth day; Christmas child. Natalie Wood, American actress. **Nathalie, Natalia, Natasha**.

Natasha a form of Natalie. Natasha Richardson, British actress.

Nathalie a form of Natalie.

Navit Hebrew: lovely.

Neala Irish: victor; a feminine form of Neal. **Neila**, **Nia**.

Neda Slavic: Sunday's child; also, Anglo-Saxon: wealthy guardian. **Nedda**, **Nedra**.

Nedra a form of Neda.

Nelda Old English: one who comes from the elder tree.

Nell a form of Helen. Nell Gwynne, 17th-century British actress, and mistress of King Charles II; Nelly Bly, American journalist. **Nelly**, **Nellie**.

Nerine Greek: ocean nymph; one who swims.

Nerissa Greek: of the ocean.

Nerys Welsh: the lord.

Nessa a form of Vanessa.

Nettie a form of Annette. **Netty**.

Nevada Latin: with lots of snow.

Nevelle a feminine form of Neville.

Nia Irish: a form of Neala.

Nicki a form of Nicole.

Nicola a form of Nicole.

Nicole Greek: triumph of the people; a feminine form of Nicholas. Nicole Kidman, Australian actress. **Nick**, **Nicki**, **Nicola**, **Nicolette**, **Nikka**.

Nicolette a form of Nicole.

Nikka a form of Nicole.

Nila Latin: Nile river. **Nilda**.

Nilda a form of Nila.

Nina Spanish: a much-loved daughter.

Nissa Scandinavian: a sociable fairy or pixie. **Nissy**.

Nolita Latin: the olive; a feminine form of Oliver.

Nona Latin: the ninth born child. **Nonie, Noni**.

Nonie a form of Nona. **Noni**.

Nora Latin: pride. Nora, character in Ibsen's play, *A Doll's House*. **Norah**.

Noreen a form of Norma.

Norma Latin: a representation; a blueprint. **Noreen**.

Norris French: from the north. Once a boy's name, increasingly used for girls.

Nurit Hebrew: small blossom.

Nyree Maori: the sea.

Nyssa Greek: the starting point; also, Latin: striving for a goal.

Nita Latin: orderly; also, Choctaw Indian: a bear.

Nitza Hebrew: a blossom.

Noa a feminine form of Noah.

Noel Latin: yuletide; a child born at Christmas. **Noelle**.

Noemi a form of Naomi.

Nola Latin: a little bell; also, Celtic: celebrated; righteous.

Noleta Latin: disinclined.

Oceane Greek: from the ocean; a goddess of the ocean. **Ocean**.

Octavia Latin: the eighth born child; a feminine form of Octavius. **Tavia**.

Odele Greek: a song. **Odelette**.

Odelette a form of Odele.

Odelia Teutonic: prosperous; well-to-do; a feminine form of Edell; also, a French patron saint. **Odile**, **Odilia**.

Odessa Greek: one who travels far.

Odetta Old French: one who makes a home livable; loyal to one's country. Odetta, American singer. **Odette**.

Odile a form of Odelia.

Odilia a form of Odelia.

Ola Old Norse: one who looks like an ancestor; a feminine form of Olaf.

Olga Teutonic: holy. Russian Grand Duchess Olga Romanov.

Olinda Latin: something that smells pleasant or agreeable.

Olive a form of Olivia. Olive Oyl, Popeye's girlfriend.

Olivia Latin: the olive; a feminine form of Oliver. **Olive**, **Olivie**.

Olivie a form of Olivia.

Olympia Greek: celestrial; from Mount Olympus.

Oma Arabic: leader; a feminine form of Omar.

Ona Latin: one. Oona O'Neil Chaplin, daughter of Eugene O'Neill, and wife of Charlie Chaplin. **Oona**, **Una**.

Ondine Latin: a swell of water.

Onyx Greek: a translucent black stone of exceptional beauty and luster.

Opal Sanskrit: the opal; a valuable gemstone.

Ophelia Greek: sagacious; eternal. Character in Shakespeare's *Hamlet*.

Oprah a form of the name Orpah. Oprah Winfrey, American talk show host.

Ora a form of Oralie.

Oralie Latin: the color of gold; the ocean coast; also, Anglo-Saxon: currency. **Oralee**, **Ora**.

Orchid New Latin: a beautiful, much-prized, and difficult to grow, three-petaled flower.

Oriana Latin: one who is the color of gold; daybreak.

Oriel Latin: golden.

Orin Greek: a form of Orina.

Orina Greek: peace. **Orin**.

Orla Irish: light.

Orli Hebrew: my illumination.

Orpah Hebrew: runaway. Letters switched to spell Oprah.

Ouida Old German: a famous warrior; a form of Louis.

Owen Celtic: youthful warrior of noble birth.

Page Anglo-Saxon: young person; childlike. **Paige**.

Palma Latin: palm tree, hand.

Palmer English: transferred use of a surname.

Paloma Spanish: dove. Paloma Picasso, French designer.

Pamela Greek: all-honey; charming; attentive; tender. **Pam, Pammie**.

Pansy Greek: the pansy flower; sweet-smelling; also, French: a thought.

Paola a form of Paula.

Papillon French: a butterfly; a small spaniel dog.

Paris French: the capital city of France on the Seine River.

Parker English: a park keeper.

Pascale Latin: relating to Easter.

Pasha Greek: from the sea.

Pat a form of Patricia.

Patience Latin: unwearied; stable strength. Patience Strong, poet.

Patricia Latin: aristocratic; born into nobility; a feminine form of Patrick. Patricia Neal, American actress. **Pat, Patty, Patti, Trish, Tricia, Trisha, Tish, Tisa, Tisha, Patrice, Patsy.**

Patrice a form of Patricia.

Patsy a form of Patricia.

Patty a form of Patricia. **Patti.**

Paula Latin: diminutive; a feminine form of Paul. **Paulette, Paulina, Pauline, Paule, Paulie, Paola.**

Paule a form of Paula.

Paulette a form of Paula. Paulette Goddard, stage name of American actress.

Paulina a form of Paula.

Pauline a form of Paula. Pauline Trigere, French designer.

Paxton Old English: from a peaceful town.

Payson Old English: transferred use of a surname.

Payton Old English: from the fighter's estate. **Peyton.**

Peaches Latin: a fruit-bearing tree of the rose family; a pet name used especially in the American South, where peach trees grow in abundance; sweet or swell person. **Peachy.**

Peachy a form of Peaches.

Pearl Latin: a pearl; a valuable gem. Pearl S. Buck, writer. **Perlie, Perri.**

Pebbles Old English: a small stone worn into a round shape by water. Pebbles Flintstone, Stone-Age cartoon baby.

Peg a form of Margaret.

Pegeen a form of Margaret.

Peggy a form of Margaret. Dame Peggy Ashcroft, actress.

Penelope Greek: one who weaves cloth or reeds. **Penny.**

Penny a form of Penelope.

Peony Greek: the peony flower; one who restores others to health.

Pepper Greek: a pungent fruit that has been used as a condiment for millennia.

Perdita Latin: lost one. From Shakespeare's *The Winter's Tale*; Pongo's canine wife in *101 Dalmatians*.

Peridot Old French: a deep yellow-green gemstone.

Perlie a form of Pearl.

Pernella Old French: a little stone; also, Celtic: a young woman; a feminine form of Peter.

Perri a form of Pearl.

Persia a country in Southeast Asia, now know as Iran.

Petal Greek: the richly colored leaf of a flower.

Petra Greek: rock; a firm foundation; a feminine form of Peter. **Piera, Petronella**.

Petronella a form of Petra.

Petula Latin: in search of. Petula Clark, British pop singer.

Petunia Native American: the petunia flower; a reddish-purple color. Porky Pig's cartoon girlfriend.

Peyton a form of Payton.

Phedra Greek: brilliant.

Philippa Greek: one who loves and cares for horses; a feminine form of Philip. Philipa Gregory, Kenyan-born British author. **Phillippine, Pippa, Pippi**.

Philomena Greek: the nightingale bird; one who adores the moon.

Phoebe Greek: light; brilliant; dazzling; sage. Phoebe Cates, American actress.

Phyllis Greek: a green branch.

Pia Italian: religious; virtuous.

Pickles Middle English: any vegetable preserved in brine or vinegar; a common American pet name.

Piera a form of Petra.

Pierrette French: firm; fixed; a feminine form of Peter.

Pilar Spanish: a pillar; groundwork.

Pinga Pakistani: dark.

Piper Old English: a pipe player.

Pippa a form of Philippa.

Pippi a form of Philippa. Fictional naughty girl, Pippi Longstocking, by Astrid Ericsson Lindgren.

Pixie English: a mischievous wood fairy; a bright, playful child.

Pleasance Middle English: delight; possessing qualities that bestow pleasure.

Plum Greek: a fruit-bearing tree of the rose family; especially sweet or desirable.

Pola Polish: a feminine form of Paul.

Polly a form of Mary.

Pomona Latin: fertile.

Poodle German: a breed of bright active dogs with a dense curly coat; a term of endearment.

Pookie English: a term of close affection.

Poopsie English: a diminutive term of endearment.

Poppy Latin: the poppy flower; perfumed.

Porter Middle English: a person posted at an entrance.

Portia Latin: a sacrifice; a swine.

Posy English: a flower or bouquet; a line of sentimental verse. **Posey.**

Precious Latin: having high value or worth.

Prentice Middle English: novice; one who is learning.

Presley English: transferred use of a surname. Elvis Presley, American musician.

Primavera Latin: the season of spring.

Primrose Latin: the first rose of the season.

Priscilla Latin: from olden times; able to trace one's line of heredity back very far. Priscilla Alden, 17th-century *Mayflower* passenger.

Prudence Latin: careful; judicious; smart; possessing prescience. **Prue.**

Prue a form of Prudence and Prunella.

Prunella Old French: prune or plum colored; purple. **Prue.**

Puddles Old English: a small pool of water; a term of endearment.

Puppy Middle French: a tame, young dog; a common term of endearment for loved ones.

Queenie a form of Quenna.

Quenby Scandinavian: a wife; like a woman.

Quenna Old English: a queen. **Queenie**.

Questa French: one who searches.

Quincy Irish: living at the house of the fifth son. Quincy Jones, American musician.

Quinn Irish: possessing wisdom and intelligence. **Quinna**, **Quinnie**.

Quinna a form of Quinn.

Quinnie a form of Quinn.

Quinta Latin: a fifth born child; a feminine form of Quentin.

Rachel Hebrew: a small lamb; placid; ingenuous; gullible. **Rachael, Rachelle, Rae, Rahel, Raquel, Rochelle, Shelley.**

Rachelle a form of Rachel.

Radella Old English: advisor.

Rae Old English: a doe; female deer.

Rain Middle English: a fall of water dropping from the sky. **Rainbow, Rainee.**

Raina Teutonic: strength; resolve; also, French-Latin: a queen.

Rainbow a form of Rain.

Rainee a form of Rain.

Raisa Russian: a rose.

Raisel Yiddish: a rose.

Ramona Teutonic: guardian; sage; fierce; a feminine form of Raymond. Ramona Quimby, girl hero of Beverly Cleary books.

Rana Sanskrit: nobility. **Ranice.**

Randy Latin: well-liked; also, Anglo-Saxon: safeguard; a feminine form of Randolf. **Randie.**

Ranice a form of Rana.

Raphaela Hebrew: a sacred person who restores others to health; healed by God; a feminine form of Raphael.

Raven Greek: a large, shiny black bird. In the Edgar Allen Poe poem of the same name, the raven is a sage but ominous bird, reminding the poet of his lost love, Lenore.

Rayanne a form of Ray and Anne.

Reagan Irish: a young person with a noble title; young monarch.

Rebecca Hebrew: bound; captivator; enchantingly beautiful. Fictional Daphne Du Maurier character in eponymous novel. **Becky, Becca, Becks, Reba, Rivka, Rifka.**

Reece Welsh: passion; zeal. Reese Witherspoon, American actress. **Reese.**

Reenie a form of Renata. **Doreen, Maureen.**

Reeve Middle English: a local bureaucrat who enforces specific regulations.

Reggie a form of Regina.

Regina Latin: a queen; like a regent. **Reggie.**

Reiko Japanese: gratitude.

Remy French: one from Rheims. **Remi.**

Rena Hebrew: a song.

Renata Latin: one who is born again. **Renate, Reenie, Rennie, Renée.**

Renée French: a form of Renata. **Reenie, Rennnie.**

Renita Latin: confident.

Reno Native American: a city in Nevada.

Reseda Latin: the mignonette flower.

Reva Latin: to recover strength or position.

Rexanna Latin: royal elegance.

Rhea Greek: coming forth from the ground; also, Latin: the poppy flower. **Rea.**

Rhoda Greek: the rose flower; one who is from Rhodes. **Rhonda, Ronni, Roni, Roney.**

Ria Spanish: the entrance of a river.

Rica Teutonic: placid river; also, Spanish: rich; something to be savored.

Richelle American: combination of Richard and Michelle.

Rihana Arabic: a sweet basil. **Rianna**.

Riley Irish: brave. **Rylee**.

Rima English: one who adores nature.

Risa Latin: mirth.

Rita Greek: a pearl. Rita Hayworth, American actress. **Margarita**.

Riva Old French: coast.

Rivka Hebrew: a form of Rebecca. **Rifka**.

Roanna Latin: kind; cordial. **Roanne, Rowen, Rowan**.

Robbie a form of Roberta.

Roberta Teutonic: dazzling notoriety; a feminine form of Robert. Roberta Flack, American singer. **Robbie, Bobbie, Bobs, Bobbette**.

Robin English: a small songbird of the thrush family.

Rochelle French: small rock.

Roderica Teutonic: celebrated princess; a feminine form of Roderick.

Rohana Hindustani: perfumed incense.

Rolanda Teutonic: from the notorious place; a feminine form of Roland.

Roma Latin: one who travels aimlessly; a woman from Rome. **Romilda**.

Romilda a form of Roma.

Romola Latin: a person from Rome. **Romy, Romilda**.

Romy a form of Romola. Romy Schneider, stage name of Austrian actress.

Ronalda Old Norse: exceedingly strong; a feminine form of Ronald. **Ronni, Roni**.

Rory Irish: a famous leader.

Rosa a form of Rose. Rosa Bonheur, French painter.

Rosabel Latin: a lovely rose.

Rosalie a form of Rose.

Rosalind English: a form of Roselinda. Shakespearean character, Rosalind.

Rosalyn a form of Roselinda.

Rosamond Teutonic: renowned guardian; one who watches over horses; also, Latin: an unsullied rose. From the 16th-century sonnet, *To Delia, the Complaint of Rosamond*.

Rosanna Latin: a refined rose.

Rose Greek: a beautiful, showy flower, the rose, cultivated from a shrub for thousands of years; love. Rose Hartwick Thorpe, poet. **Rosie, Rosy, Rosa, Roseann, Roseanne, Rosemarie, Rosemary, Ro, Rosalie, Rosalyn, Rosalind, Rosabel, Rosina**.

Roseann a form of Rose and Ann.

Roseanne a form of Rose and Anne.

Roselinda Spanish: a lovely rose. **Rosalyn, Roslyn**.

Rosemarie a form of Rose and Marie.

Rosemary a form of Rose and Mary.

Rosette Italian: small rose. **Rosetta, Rosita**.

Rosie a form of Rose.

Rosina Italian: a form of Rose.

Roslyn a form of Roselinda.

Ross Teutonic: horse; peninsula; red.

Rowan a form of Roanna.

Rowena Celtic: long white hair; also, Anglo-Saxon: celebrated friend.

Roxana a form of Roxanne.

Roxanne Persian: daybreak. **Roxy, Roxana**.

Roxy a form of Roxanne.

Ruby Latin: a precious gemstone; red. Ruby Keeler, American singer and dancer.

Rudelle Teutonic: eminence.

Rudy Teutonic: legendary wolf.

Rue Greek: an herb of grace.

Rufina Greek: redheaded; a feminine form of Rufus.

Rusty Latin: redheaded; also, Anglo-Saxon: like a fox.

Ruth Hebrew: lovely friend; empathetic. Ruth Gordon, American actress.

Ryan Irish: a prince.

S

Sabina Latin: a woman of Sabine, a place in ancient Italy. **Sabine, Binnie**.

Sabine a form of Sabina.

Sabra Hebrew: to take a break.

Sabrina Latin: one who is from the border; also, Anglo-Saxon: a princess.

Sacha Greek: one who assists humanity; also, Russian: a feminine form of Alexander.

Sachi Japanese: blissful.

Sachiko Japanese: blissful child.

Sadie a form of Sarah.

Sadira Persian: the lotus tree; pensive; also, Arabic: an ostrich returning from the water.

Saffron Arabic: a deep yellow-orange stigma of a type of crocus, used as a pungent seasoning and coloring in Spanish and other cuisines. Saffy Monsoon, long-suffering daughter in British comedy, *Absolutely Fabulous*. **Saffy**.

Sage Middle English: wise; knowing; possessing good judgment; a European perennial mint.

Sailor Old English: a mariner; one who travels by water.

Sakura Japanese: a cherry blossom.

Sal a form of Sarah.

Salina Greek: salty.

Sally a form of Sarah. Sally Bowles, character in *Cabaret*.

Salome Hebrew: stillness; serenity.

Sam a form of Samantha.

Samantha Aramaic: one who listens; considerate. **Sam**.

Sancia Latin: holy; pure.

Sandra a form of Alexandra. Sandra Day O'Connor, first woman American Supreme Court Justice. **Sandy, Sandi**.

Sandy a form of Alexandra.

Sapphire Greek: a deep blue gem; blue; also, Hebrew: beautiful.

Sara a form of Sarah.

Sarah Jane a form of Sarah and Jane.

Sarah Hebrew: a princess. Sarah Bernhardt, French actress. **Sara, Sal, Sally, Sadie, Sari, Zara**.

Sari a form of Sarah.

Sarita Hebrew: a young princess.

Sascha a form of Alexandra.

Satin Arabic: a fine, silky fabric with a shiny and a dull side.

Savanna Old Spanish: one who is from the mesa or open field. **Savannah**.

Sayo Japanese: one who is born at night.

Scarlet Middle English: a deep red color. Scarlett O'Hara, Margaret Mitchell's character from *Gone with the Wind*. **Scarlett**.

Schyler a form of Skylar.

Scottie Latin: one who is from Scotland; one who is tattooed.

Scout Latin: one sent to obtain information; explore. Scout was the sister in Harper Lee's novel, *To Kill A Mockingbird*.

Season Middle English: a period of time usually characterized by a particular kind of weather. Season Hubley, American actress.

Seaton English: transferred use of a surname.

Sebastiana Greek: great; venerated; a feminine form of Sebastian.

Sela Hebrew: a rock. Sela Ward, American actress.

Selby English: a willow farm.

Selena Greek: the moon. **Celine, Céline.**

Selima Hebrew: serene; also, Arabic: a feminine form of Solomon.

Selma Teutonic: guarded; celestial shield; also, Celtic: light colored; a feminine form of Anselm. Selma Blair, American actress.

Semele Latin: only once.

Senalda Spanish: a premonition.

Seneca Native American: an Iroquois tribe.

Septima Latin: seventh-born child.

Sequoia Native American: a giant, coniferous California tree.

Seraphina Hebrew: fervent; zealous. **Serafina, Saraina.**

Serena Latin: composed; placid; still. Serena Stevens, Samantha's cousin on *Bewitched*, played by Elizabeth Montgomery. **Sarina.**

Serenity Latin: very peaceful.

Shalyn African-American: created name.

Shana Irish: a form of the name Jane; also, Hebrew: God is gracious and good.

Shanika African-American: created name. **Shanequa.**

Shanna a form of Shannon.

Shannon Irish: small, wise one. **Shanna.**

Shantae a form of Chantal. **Shantay.**

Shari a form of Sharon. Shari Lewis, American puppeteer.

Sharon Hebrew: unusual loveliness; the plain of Sharon. Sharon Stone, American actress. **Shari, Sherona, Sharona.**

Shawna Irish: a contemporary form of Sean; a form of John. **Shauna.**

Shea Hebrew: asked for.

Sheba Hebrew: from Sheba; the daughter of our promise.

Sheena Irish: a present from God.

Sheila Celtic: tuneful. **Shayla**.

Shelby Old English: from the village of the willow trees.

Shelley Old English: an island with lots of shells.

Sherika Arabic: an Easterner.

Sherilyn a form of Cheryl and Lynn.

Sherman Anglo-Saxon: one who shaves sheep; one who cuts cloth.

Sherona a form of Sharon. **Sharona**.

Sherry French: treasured. **Cherie**, **Sheri**.

Sheryl a form of Cheryl.

Shevon a form of Siobhan. **Shavonne**.

Shira Hebrew: a song.

Shirley Anglo-Saxon: from the white pasture. Shirley Temple, child star.

Shizu Japanese: quiet and clear.

Shoshana Hebrew: a rose.

Sian Welsh: Jane.

Sibyl Greek: a prophet. **Sybil, Cybil, Cybill, Cybille**.

Sidonia Phoenician: to trap; also, Greek: linen. **Sidonie**.

Sidra Latin: one who is of the stars; dazzling.

Sienna Italian: a red-brown pigment made from burning oxidized earth.

Sierra Irish: black one; also, Spanish: a mountain range with a jagged shape. **Ciara**.

Sigfreda Old German: success; realization of a goal; inner peace; a feminine form of Siegfried.

Silja Scandinavian: a form of Cecilia.

Silver English: the precious metal of the same name, sometimes used for babies born with very light-colored hair.

Simone Hebrew: one who listens; a feminine form of Simon. Simone Signoret, German-born French actress; Simone de Beauvoir, French writer.

Siobhan Irish: a form of Jane. **Shevon**, **Shavonne**.

Sister Sanskrit: a female sibling. **Sis**, **Sissy**, **Cissy**.

Sita Sanskrit: a gully in which farms are planted; the Hindu goddess of agriculture and the harvest. **Sitta**.

Sky a form of Skylar.

Skylar Dutch: a scholar; shelter. **Skyler**, **Sky**, **Schyler**.

Sloan Celtic: a warrior. **Sloane**.

Sofia Greek: sagacity. Sofia Loren, Italian actress. **Sophia**, **Sophie**.

Solange French: serious; pious. St. Solange was killed for resisting her master's attempts to corrupt her virtue.

Soleil French: the sun. Soleil Moon Fry, American actress.

Sondra Greek: one who helps humanity.

Sonia Greek: a foreigner. Sonia Braga, Brazilian actress. **Sonja**, **Sonya**.

Sook Korean: pure.

Sophia a form of Sofia.

Sophie a form of Sofia.

Sophronia Greek: sage; rational; shrewd.

Spencer Middle English: one who supplies necessities.

Spring Old English: the season between winter and summer.

Stacey Greek: one who will rise again; to restore to life; to live forever. **Stacy**, **Stacia**.

Star Anglo-Saxon: a bright, shining luminous body visible in the night sky.

Steffi a form of Stephanie.

Stella Latin: a star.

Stephania a form of Stephanie.

Stephanie Greek: a coronet; a wreath; a feminine form of Stephen. **Steffi**, **Stephania**, **Stevie**.

Stevie a form of Stephanie.

Stockard Middle English: one who lives near a footbridge. Stockard Channing, stage name of American actress.

Storm Old English: stormy; tempestuous. **Stormy**.

Sue a form of Susan.

Sukey a form of Susan.

Summer Sanskrit: the season between spring and autumn.

Sunny English: of a bright disposition; positive.

Susan Hebrew: a lily flower. **Sue, Susie, Susanna, Susannah, Suzanne, Suzette, Suesue, Susu, Sukey, Swoosie.**

Susanna a form of Susan. **Susannah.**

Susie a form of Susan.

Susu a form of Susan.

Suzanne a form of Susan.

Suzette a form of Susan.

Swanhilda Teutonic: a female swan fighter.

Sweetie Old English: marked by gentle good humor or kindliness.

Swoosie a form of Susan. Swoosie Kurtz, American actress.

Sybil a form of Sibyl.

Sydelle Hebrew: one who enthralls.

Sydney Hebrew: tempter; a feminine form of Sidney.

Sylvia Latin: a young woman of the woods. Sylvia Plath, American poet. **Sylvie, Sylvain.**

Syreeta Arabic: a companion.

Tabby a form of Tabitha.

Tabitha Aramaic: the gazelle; poised. Tabitha Soren, MTV personality. **Tabby**.

Tace a form of Tacy.

Tacita Latin: unspoken.

Tacy Latin: be silent; a common name for the Puritans. **Tace, Tayce, Taisy**.

Taffy English: a pulled candy made of brown sugar or molasses.

Tai a form of Tiana.

Taisy a form of Tacy.

Tal a form of Talia.

Tala a form of Talia.

Talbot Norman: a large breed of bloodhound.

Talcott English: transferred use of a surname.

Talia Hebrew: heaven's dew. Talia Shire, American actress. **Tal, Tala, Tali**.

Tallulah Native American: leaping water; lively. Tallulah Bankhead, American actress.

Tama Hebrew: incredulousness. Tama Janowitz, American writer.

Tamar a form of Tamara.

Tamara Hebrew: a palm tree. **Tamar, Tamra**.

Tameko Japanese: child of goodness. **Tamiko, Tamika**.

Tammy Hebrew: flawlessness. Tammy Wynette, American country singer.

Tamra a form of Tamara.

Tamsin English: from Thomas; a twin. **Tamsyn**.

Tansy Latin: dogged; determined.

Tanya Slavic: a fairy queen. Tanya Tucker, American country singer. **Tania**.

Tao Chinese: a peach.

Tara Irish: a tower made of rough rocks; peak; ancient capital of Irish kings. **Taryn**.

Taryn a form of Tara.

Tatiana Russian: from a Roman family name of obscure origin.

Tatum Middle English: cheerful one. Tatum O'Neal, American actress.

Tawny Middle English: a warm, light brown color.

Tayce a form of Tacy.

Taylor Latin: tailor; one who modifies.

Teagan a form of Tegan.

Teal English: a variety of small duck; blue.

Tegan Celtic: doe. **Teagan**.

Temperance Latin: in moderation; balance.

Tempest Old French: passionate; stormy. Tempest Bledsoe, American actress.

Teresa a form of Theresa.

Teresina Italian: a form of Theresa.

Teresita a form of Theresa.

Terri a form of Theresa.

Terry a form of Theresa.

Tertia Latin: a third born child. **Tia, Tea, Teah**.

Tess a form of Tessa. *Tess of the d'Urbervilles*, by Thomas Hardy. **Tessie**.

Tessa Greek: a fourth born child. **Tess, Tessie**.

Tetty a form of Charlotte.

Thaddea Greek: exalted; valorous; a feminine form of Thaddeus.

Thalassa Greek: from the ocean.

Thea Greek: godly; amazingly lovely.

Thecia Greek: celestial renown.

Theda Greek: a present from God. Theda Bara, stage name of American actress.

Thee a form of Theodora.

Thelma Greek: one who is still nursing. Thelma and Louise, film heroines.

Themis Greek: fairness; justice. **Thema**.

Theodora Greek: a holy gift from God; a feminine form of Theodore. **Thea, Thee**.

Theodosia Greek: God-given.

Theola Greek: one who communicated with divinity.

Theone Greek: heavenly.

Theophila Greek: one who is loved by God.

Theora Greek: one who meditates.

Thera Greek: untamed; feral.

Theresa Greek: one who harvests. **Teresa, Terry, Terri, Therese, Tresa, Tressie, Trea, Tersina, Teresita**.

Therese a form of Theresa.

Thora Old Norse: thunder; a feminine form of Thor. Thora Birch, American actress.

Tia a form of Tertia. Tea Leone, American actress. **Tea, Teah**.

Tiana Greek: a princess. **Tai**.

Tiberia Latin: from the Tiber River. **Tibbie**.

Tiffany Greek: from the viewpoint of the divinity. **Tiffy, Tiff**.

Tiffy a form of Tiffany.

Tilda a form of Matilda.

Tillie a form of Matilda.

Timothea Greek: one who exalts the divinity; a feminine form of Timothy. **Timee**.

Tina a form of Christina or Martina. Tina Turner, American singer.

Tinka Middle English: variant of Tinkle; sound of bells.

Tinsley English: transferred use of a surname.

Tippi a form of Ziporah. Tippi Hedren, American actress. **Tippy**.

Tirza Hebrew: a cypress tree.

Tisa Swahili: the ninth-born child. Tisa Farrow, American actress.

Tish a form of Patricia.

Tisha a form of Patricia.

Tita Latin: a title of honor.

Titania Greek: titan; giant. **Tania**, **Tita**.

Toby Hebrew: God is good; a feminine form of Tobias. **Tovah**, **Tova**.

Tomasina Aramaic: a twin; a feminine form of Thomas. **Tommie**.

Toni Latin: beyond worth or praise; a short form of Antoinette.

Topaz Latin: the topaz gem.

Topsy English: askew.

Tori a form of Victoria. Tori Amos, stage name of American singer and songwriter.

Totsi Native American: moccasins. **Totsy**.

Tottie a form of Charlotte.

Tourmaline Singhalese: the tourmaline gem.

Tovah a form of Toby. Tovah Feldshuh, American actress. **Tova**.

Tracey Norman: transferred use of a surname, from the baronial place name; also, Greek: summer. **Tracie**.

Trea a familiar form of Theresa.

Tresa a form of Theresa.

Tressie a form of Theresa.

Trilby Italian: to sing with trills; frolicsome.

Trina Greek: limpidness.

Trinette Greek: small pure one.

Trinity Latin: three; name taken in honor of the Christian Holy Trinity.

Trish a form of Patricia.

Trista Latin: sorrowful; a feminine form of Tristen.

Tristan a form of the masculine names Tristen and Tristram. **Trista**.

Trixie Latin: a boon; one who brings joy.

Trudy Old German: loved one; a short form of Gertrude.

True Middle English: unwavering; unswerving.

Tucker Old English: one who tucks or folds cloth.

Tuesday Old English: born on Tuesday. Tuesday Weld, stage name of American actress.

Tula Hindi: born under the sign of Libra.

Tullia Irish: still; placid; demure; a feminine form of Tully.

Twyla English: a weave of double thread. Twyla Tharp, American dancer and choreographer.

Tyler Anglo-Saxon: one who fashions bricks or tiles.

Tyne English: a river. Tyne Daily, American actress.

Tyra Scandinavian: Thor battler.

Tziporah a form of Ziporah.

Udele Anglo-Saxon: very rich.

Ula Teutonic: an heir to an estate; also, Celtic: a jewel from the ocean.

Ulrica Teutonic: leader of all; a feminine form of Ulric.

Uma Sanskrit: flax or turmeric. From Indian mythology, this name is said to derive from the contraction of the words "O do not." Uma Thurman, American actress.

Una a form of Ona. **Oona**.

Undine Latin: a wave; a water sprite. **Ondine**.

Ursa Latin: a female bear.

Ursel Latin: a small female bear.

Ursula Latin: female bear; intrepid. Ursula Andress, Swiss-born actress.

Uta Teutonic: a heroine in battle. Uta Hagen, German-born actress.

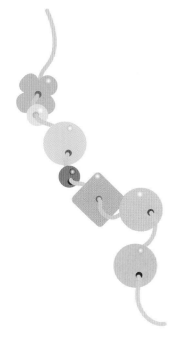

Val a form of Valentine and Valerie.

Vala Gothic: the chosen one.

Valda Teutonic: a heroine in battle.

Valeda Latin: dynamic; possessing a strong body.

Valentine Latin: brave; vivacious; fortitude. **Val, Valentina, Tina**.

Valentina a form of Valentine.

Valerie Latin: brave; strapping. **Val**.

Valonia Latin: one who is from the vale or valley.

Valora Latin: courageous.

Vanda a form of Wanda.

Vanessa Greek: butterfly. Vanessa Noel, American fashion designer. **Nessa**.

Vania Hebrew: a present from the divinity; a Russian feminine form of John.

Vanora Old Welsh: a surging wave.

Vashti Persian: lovely.

Veda Sanskrit: erudition; sagacity.

Vedette Italian: a sentry; also, French: a film star.

Vega Arabic: a falling star.

Velda Teutonic: the insight of inspiration.

Velika Slavic: one who is grand.

Velma Teutonic: a strong guardian; the helmet; a feminine form of William.

Velvet Middle English: a soft, plush fabric.

Ventura Spanish: fortuitous.

Venus Latin: splendor; the Roman goddess of beauty.

Vera Latin: faithful; accurate.

Verbena Latin: the flower verbena.

Verda Latin: novel; original.

Verena Old German: protector.

Verna Latin: vernal; one who is born in the spring.

Veronica Latin-Greek: an accurate depiction. Fictional comic book heroine. **Veronique.**

Veronique a form of Veronica.

Vespera Latin: evening star.

Vesta Latin: one who stays at home.

Vicky a form of Victoria.

Victoire a form of Victoria.

Victoria Latin: winning; a feminine form of Victor. **Vicky, Vicki, Victoire, Tori.**

Vida Hebrew: one who is well loved. **Vita.**

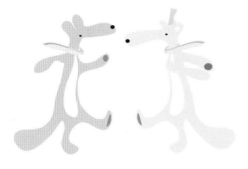

Vidonia Portuguese: a bough of a vine.

Vigilia Latin: attentive; pensive; watchful.

Vignette French: a small vine.

Villette French: a small town.

Vincentia Latin: triumphant; a feminine form of Vincent. **Vincenta**, **Vincenza**, **Vin**.

Vinita Latin: a woman from Venice.

Vinna Anglo-Saxon: of the vine.

Viola Italian: one who plays the musical instrument called a viol.

Violet Latin: the gilly flower, which is purple-blue, this flower symbolizes shyness and modesty. Violet Paget, British wrtier. **Vi**, **Violette**, **Violetta**.

Virgilia Latin: alive; one who carries a rod or staff.

Virginia Latin: virginal; self-possessed and strong. Virginia Woolf, British writer; Virginia Dare, first child of English descent born in 16th-century North America. **Virginie**, **Ginger**, **Ginny**, **Virgy**.

Virginie French: a form of Virginia.

Viridas Latin: blossoming; young.

Vita Latin: life; vivacious.

Viveca Swedish: war fortress. Viveca Lindfors, Swedish-born actress.

Vivian Latin: full of energy. Vivian Vance, American actress. **Viv**, **Vivi**, **Viviana**.

Viviana Italian: a form of Vivian.

Voletta Old French: veiled.

Wahkuna Native American: lovely.

Walda Old German: ruler; a feminine form of Waldo.

Walker English: one who walks.

Wallis Old English: one who is from Wales; a feminine form of Wallace. Wallis Simpson, Duchess of Windsor. **Wally**.

Wanda Teutonic: one who walks far and wide. **Vanda**.

Wanetta Anglo-Saxon: one who is light-skinned.

Warda Old German: a woman who watches over; guardian; a feminine form of Ward.

Wednesday Old English: the fourth day of the week. Wednesday, Charles Addams's fictional daughter in *The Addams Family*.

Welcome Anglo-Saxon: a salutation; to greet happily.

Wenda a form of Wendy.

Wendelin a form of Gwendolyn.

Wendy a form of Gwendolyn. Peter Pan's girl in J. M. Barrie's *Peter Pan*. **Wenda**.

Wenona Native American: a first-born child. Winona Ryder, stage name of American actress. **Winona**.

Wesley Old English: from the westward pasture. **Wesla, Wesa**.

Whitney Middle English: by the white island. Whitney Blake, American actress.

Wilda Anglo-Saxon: feral; crude.

Wilfreda Teutonic: arbitrator. **Freda, Freddie**.

Wilhelmina Teutonic: a strong guardian; a feminine form of William. **Willa, Willi, Willie, Willow, Wilma, Mina, Minette, Minnie, Minerva, Minka**.

Willa a form of Wilhelmina.

Willette English: a form of William.

Willi a form of Wilhelmina.

Willie a form of Wilhelmina.

Willow English: willow tree.

Wilma a form of Wilhelmina.

Wilona Anglo-Saxon: advantageous.

Windy a form of Gwendolyn.

Winifred English: blessed reunion. **Winnie, Winkie, Winkle, Freddie**.

Winkie a form of Winifred.

Winkle a form of Winifred.

Winnie a form of Winifred and Gwendolyn.

Winola Old German: genial; welcoming.

Winter Old English: the season between autumn and spring.

Wren Old English: a small singing bird.

Wynn a form of Gwendolyn. **Wynne**.

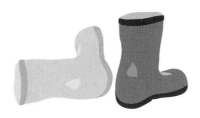

Xanthe Greek: golden-haired.

Xaviera Arabic: brilliant; a feminine form of Xavier.

Xena Greek: a foreigner.

Xenia Greek: friendly.

Xylia Greek: from the forest.

Xylona Greek: of the woods.

Yael Hebrew: a female wild goat.

Yaffa Hebrew: lovely.

Yardley English: from the enclosed meadow. Yeardley Smith, American actress. **Yeardley, Yard**.

Yasmin Persian: the jasmine flower; a perfumed blossom. **Yasmine, Jasmin**.

Yedda Old English: one who writes or sings songs.

Yelena a form of Helena.

Yetta Old English: a philanthropist.

Yolanda Greek: the violet flower; modest. **Yolande, Iolanthe**.

Yolande a form of Yolanda.

Yonah Hebrew: a dove.

Yseult Celtic: the light one.

Yuki Japanese: lucky one; snow. **Yukiko**.

Yvette French: a familiar form of Yvonne. Yvette Mimieux, American actress. **Evette, Ivette**.

Yvonne Old French: a feminine form of Ivar; a user of the yew-bow. **Evonne, Lavonne, Yvette, Evette**.

Zabrina Anglo-Saxon: of aristocratic birth. **Brina**, **Zabrine**.

Zandra Greek: one who aids humanity; a feminine form of Alexander. Zandra Rhodes, British fashion designer.

Zara Hebrew: morning radiance. **Zaro**.

Zaro a form of Zara.

Zea Latin: like mature grain.

Zebada Hebrew: a present from the divinity; a feminine form of Zebadiah. **Zeba**.

Zena Persian: a female person.

Zenobia Arabic: a father's delight. **Zenobie**.

Zera Hebrew: a kernel that is planted for harvest.

Zerelda Teutonic: a woman who goes into battle.

Zerlina Teutonic: serene; lovely.

Zeta Greek: the letter "Z."

Zillah Hebrew: silhouette; depiction.

Zinnia Latin: the zinnia flower.

Zipporah Hebrew: a sparrow, or small gray or brown songbird. **Tzipporah**, **Tzippy**, **Ceporah**, **Tippi**, **Tippy**, **Zippora**.

Zita Celtic: tempting.

Zizi Hungarian: an endearment for Elizabeth.

Zoë Greek: life. Zoë Akins, author.

Zora Slavic: daybreak. Zora Neale Hurston, American writer.

Zuleika Arabic: the light one.

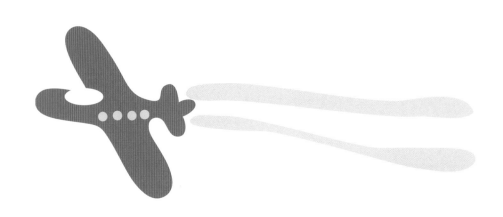

Boys' Names

Aaron Hebrew: mountain, light. **Aron**.

Abbott Hebrew: father. **Abbot**.

Abdul Arabic: a servant of Allah. **Abdullah**.

Abe a short a form of Abraham.

Abel Hebrew: breath of vanity.

Abner Hebrew: lamp of light. Abbie Hoffman, counterculture icon and author. **Ab, Abbie, Avner**.

Abraham Hebrew: exalted father of multitudes. Abraham Lincoln, 16th American president. **Abe, Abie, Abram, Avram, Bram**.

Abram a short form of Abraham.

Ace Latin: unity.

Adair Celtic: from the ford near the oak tree.

Adam Hebrew: man of the red earth. **Addie, Addy, Keddy**.

Addie a form of Adam.

Addison Saxon: a descendant of Adam.

Addy a form of Adam.

Adler Old English: eagle.

Adrian Latin: dark one; also, Greek: wealthy, great. **Adrien.**

Ahmed Arabic: most praised. Ahmad Rashad, American athlete and sportscaster. **Ahmad, Ahmet.**

Aidan Irish: little, fiery one. Aidan Quinn, American actor. **Aiden.**

Ainsley Scottish and English: transferred use of a surname. **Ainslie, Ainslee.**

Ajax Greek: mythical warrior.

Ajay Pakistani: victorious one. **A.J.**

Akil Arabic: thoughtful.

Alan Celtic: handsome, cheerful. **Al, Alain, Allan, Allen.**

Alaric English: transferred use of a surname.

Alasdair Scottish and Irish: a form of Alexander. Alistair Cook, British television presenter. **Alastair, Alisdair.**

Albert Saxon: noble. Prince Albert of Saxe-Coburg-Gotha, husband of British Queen Victoria. **Al, Albie, Alberto, Bert, Bertie.**

Alden Anglo-Saxon: old friend, protector. **Aldin, Elden, Eldin.**

Aldo Saxon: rich and wise. **Al.**

Alec Greek: a form of Alexander.

Alejandro Spanish: a form of Alexander. Alejandro Rey, Argentinian-born actor. **Handro.**

Aleron Latin: friend in battle.

Alexander Greek: protector. **Al, Alex, Alec, Alexi, Alasdair, Alastair, Alessandro, Alexandre, Alejandro, Alexis, Sanders, Saunders, Sandy, Sascha, Sasha, Xander, Zander.**

Alexi Russian: a form of Alexander.

Alfred Anglo-Saxon: a wise elf. **Al, Alfredo, Alfie, Fred, Freddy, Fredo.**

Algernon French: whiskered one. **Al, Algie, Algy, Alger.**

Alonso Italian: a form of Alphonse.

Alonzo Spanish: a form of Alphonse.

Aloysisus English: a form of Louis.

Alphonse Saxon: fighter. **Alfonso, Alonso, Alonzo, Lon, Lonnie, Lonny.**

Alston Anglo-Saxon: one from the old village. **Al, Alton.**

Alton English: transferred use of a surname.

Alvin Saxon: a friend to all. Alvin, cartoon chipmunk. **Alvy**, **Al**, **Elvin**.

Amadeus Latin: love of God. Wolfgang Amadeus Mozart, Austrian composer.

Amedeo Italian: a form of Amadeus. Amedeo Modigliani, Italian-Jewish painter.

Ambert Saxon: the bright one.

Ambrose Latin: immortal.

Ames French: a friend.

Amir Hebrew: it is proclaimed; also Arabic: prince.

Amory Latin: loved one. **Amery**, **Emory**.

Amos Hebrew: burden.

Anatole Greek: from the East. Anatole France, pen-name of 19th-century writer Jacques Anatole Thibault. **Anatol**.

Anders Scandinavian: a form of Andrew.

André French and Portuguese: a form of Andrew.

Andreas Greek: a form of Andrew.

Andrew Greek: strong. **Anders**, **Andreas**, **André**, **Andy**, **Drew**.

Angel a form of Angelo.

Angelo Greek: angelic. **Angel**.

Angus Celtic: strong. **Gus**, **Gussie**.

Ansel a form of Anselm. Ansel Adams, American photographer.

Anselm Saxon: a helmet from God. **Ansel**.

Anson Anglo-Saxon: son of Ann.

Anthony Latin: one who is beyond worth or praise. **Anton**, **Antonio**, **Antony**, **Tony**, **Antoine**.

Antoine French: a form of Anthony.

Anton Russian and German: a form of Anthony.

Antonio Spanish and Italian: a form of Anthony. Antonio Banderas, Spanish-born actor.

Antony a form of Anthony.

Archer a form of Archibald.

Archibald Saxon: bold prince. Archibald Leach, actor Cary Grant's real name. **Archer, Archie.**

Arden Latin: sincere, fiery.

Ari Hebrew: lion. **Arie, Arieh.**

Armand Old German: armed man.

Armstrong English and Scottish: transferred use of a surname.

Arnaud French: a form of Arnold.

Arnold Saxon: strong like an eagle. Arnold Palmer, American golfer. **Arn, Arnie, Arno, Arnaud.**

Arthur Celtic: strong like a rock. Arthur Miller, American playwright. **Art, Artie, Artur.**

Arvid Scandinavian: eagle in a tree. **Arvad.**

Asa Hebrew: healer.

Ash Old English: ash tree. **Ashby.**

Ashby Scandinavian: a form of Ash.

Asher Hebrew: laughing boy; lucky one.

Ashford Anglo-Saxon: one who lives near the ash tree.

Ashley Old English: from the ash tree meadow.

Ashton Old English: from the ash tree farm.

Aston English: transferred use of a surname. **Astin.**

Atlas Greek: carrier.

Aubrey French: king of the elves; blond one. **Bree**.

Auden English: friend. Audie Murphy, American war hero and movie cowboy. **Audie**.

Audric French: wise ruler.

August Latin: majestic. **Augie, Augus, Auguste, Augustine, Augustus, Gus, Gussie**.

Augustine a form of August.

Augustus Latin: magnificent. **August, Augustine, Augustin, Gus**.

Austin English: transferred use of a surname.

Averell Anglo-Saxon: born in April; also, Old English: one who kills wild boar.

Avery Anglo-Saxon: ruler of elves.

Avi Hebrew: father.

Avner Hebrew: a form of Abner.

Avram a form of Abraham.

Axel Old German: little oak tree. Axel Rose, musician's stage name.

Bailey Old French: steward.

Baines English: transferred use of a surname.

Baird Celtic: a musician who travels. **Bard**.

Baker Old English: a baker.

Baldwin Saxon: protector.

Bancroft Saxon: bean grower.

Banning Celtic: little blond one.

Barclay Scottish: birch tree.

Barden Scottish: from the small valley where barley grows.

Barlow English: transferred use of a surname.

Barnabas a form of Barnaby.

Barnaby Hebrew: prophetic. Barnaby Jones, fictional television sleuth. **Barnabas, Barney**.

Barnes English: from the name of a place.

Barnett English: from the name of a place called Barnet.

Baron Old English: a warrior. Barron Hilton, hotelier. **Barron**.

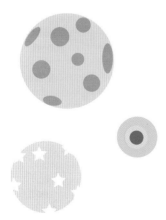

Barret Saxon: strong like a bear. **Barrett**.

Barry Celtic: spear.

Bartholomew Hebrew: farmer. Bart Simpson, cartoon bad boy. **Bart**, **Barth**, **Bat**.

Barton Anglo-Saxon: a farmer. **Bart**.

Basil Latin: a magnificent king. Basil Rathbone, South African-born actor.

Bastien a form of Sebastian.

Baxter Saxon: baker.

Bayard Old French: a horse trainer.

Beasley Old English: from the field of peas.

Beau Old French: handsome one. **Bo**.

Beaumont French: from the beautiful mountain.

Beauregard French: handsome. **Beau**, **Bo**.

Beck Old Norse and English: small stream.

Becker English: transferred use of a surname.

Belden Old English: child of an unspoiled glen. **Beldon**.

Bell Latin: beautiful.

Bellamy Latin: a beautiful friend. **Bell**.

Ben a short form of Benjamin.

Benedict Latin: blessed one. Benedick, character in Shakespeare's *Much Ado About Nothing*. **Benedick**, **Ben**, **Bennett**, **Benny**, **Dixon**.

Benjamin Hebrew: son of the right hand. Benjamin Franklin, 18th-century inventor, writer, statesman, and philosopher. **Ben**, **Benjy**, **Benny**, **Benson**, **Benedict**, **Jamie**, **Bennett**, **Benno**, **Benoît**, **Benson**.

Bennett English: a form of Benedict.

Benno German: a bear.

Benoît French: a form of Benjamin.

Benson English: the name of a place.

Bentley English: from the clearing.

Benton Anglo-Saxon: from the moors. **Ben.**

Berkeley Anglo-Saxon: from the birch meadow. **Barclay, Berkley.**

Bernard Anglo-Saxon: brave as a bear. Bernard M. Baruch, American financier and writer. **Bernie, Bern, Bernardo.**

Bertram Latin: a brilliant raven. **Bert, Bertie, Bertrand.**

Bertrand French: a form of Bertram.

Bevan Welsh: well-born, noble. **Bevin.**

Bing German: one who is from the hollow. Bing Crosby, American singer. **Bingo.**

Bingo a form of Bing.

Bink Latin: to conquer. **Binky.**

Bishop Old English: bishop.

Bjorn Swedish: bear. Björn Borg, Swedish tennis great.

Blackburn Scottish: from the dark brook. **Black.**

Blade Old English: the prosperous one, glory.

Blaine Irish: lean one. **Blain, Blane, Blayne.**

Blair Irish: of the field; also, French: a patron saint. Blair Underwood, American actor.

Blaise Latin: stutterer. **Blaze.**

Blake Old English: fair.

Blue Latin: the name of a color.

Bobby a form of Robert.

Boden Old French: messenger. **Bodie.**

Bodie a form of Boden.

Bogart Irish: soft marshy place.

Bond Old English: soil tiller.

Boone Old Norse: a blessing. Daniel Boone, American frontiersman.

Booth Teutonic: lover of home. **Boots.**

Boris Slavic: warrior.

Bosley Middle English: a thicket. **Boston, Boswell.**

Boston a form of Bosley.

Boswell a form of Bosley. James Boswell, 18th-century Scottish essayist.

Bowen Celtic: well-born. **Bowie**.

Bowie a form of Bowen. Bowie Kuhn, commissioner of American baseball.

Boyce Old French: the son of the forest.

Boyd Celtic: blond.

Brad Anglo-Saxon: wide. Brad Pitt, American actor.

Braden a form of Bradley.

Bradford Anglo-Saxon: of the broad river. **Brad**.

Bradley Anglo-Saxon: of the broad meadow. **Brad**, **Braden**.

Brady Irish: transferred use of a surname.

Bram Dutch: a form of Abraham.

Brandon English: transferred use of a surname. Brandon Cruz, American actor.

Brant Teutonic: fiery.

Breckin Irish: transferred use of a surname. Breckin Meyer, American actor.

Breeze English: transferred use of a surname.

Brendan Celtic: fiery light. Brendan Fraser, American actor. **Branen**, **Brandon**, **Brendon**, **Brennan**.

Brennan English: a raven.

Brent Old English: steep.

Brett Celtic: from Brittany. **Bret**.

Brian Celtic: strong, virtuous leader. **Bryan**, **Bryant**, **Byron**.

Brice Celtic: quick-witted. Brice Marsden, American painter. **Bryce**.

Brighton English: from the name of a place.

Brock Old English: a badger.

Broderick Teutonic: prince. Broderick Crawford, American actor. **Derrick**, **Roderick**.

Brody Scottish: from a muddy place. **Brodie**.

Bronson Old English: the darker one. Bronson Pinchot, American actor.

Brooks English: one who dwells by the brook. Harold Brooks-Baker, British director of *Burke's Peerage*.

Brown English: from the name of a color.

Bruce Old French: from the thickets. Bruce Springsteen, American musician.

Bruno Teutonic: brown-haired. Bruno Kirby, stage name of American actor.

Bryant English: transferred use of a surname. Bryant Gumbel, American television personality.

Bryce a form of Brice.

Bubba German: a boy; a term of endearment. Bubba Crosby, American baseball player.

Buck Old English: swift and graceful as a deer. Buck Henry, stage name of an American actor; Bucky Dent, American baseball player. **Buckey, Bucky, Buckley.**

Budd Old English: herald. **Bud, Buddy.**

Buddy a form of Budd.

Burke Teutonic: one who lives in the castle. **Berg, Berger, Bergess.**

Burnett English: from the name of a place.

Burton Anglo-Saxon: famous. **Burt, Bert, Berton.**

Busby Scottish: a village in the bushes. Busby Berkeley, American choreographer and film director. **Buzz.**

Buster English: a nickname. Buster Keaton, American comedian and filmmaker.

Butch English: nickname for a butcher. Butch Cassidy, American outlaw.

Buzz a form of Busby. Buzz Aldrin, American astronaut.

Byron Old French: bear-like. **Biron.**

Cabot English: transferred use of a surname.

Cade English: transferred use of a surname.

Caesar Latin: blue-eyed ruler. Cesar Chavez, Mexican-American migrant worker organizer. **Cesar**.

Calder Old English: the cool, clear spring.

Caldwell Old English: from the cool, clear well.

Caleb Hebrew: faithful and bold. **Cal**, **Cale**.

Callahan Irish: little, feisty one. **Cal**, **Callie**, **Calhoun**.

Calvin Latin: bald. Calvin Trillin, American humorist and author; Calvin Coolidge, 29th American president. **Cal**, **Callie**.

Camden Scottish: from the winding valley.

Cameron Celtic: individual. **Cam**.

Campbell Scottish: transferred use of a surname. Campbell Scott, American actor.

Cary Old Welsh: one who lives at the castle. Cary Grant, stage name of the British-born actor. **Carey**.

Carl German: a version of Charles.
Carleton, **Carlton**, **Carlisle**, **Carlyle**,
Carlo, **Carlos**.

Carleton German: farm dweller.
Carlton, television doorman on
Rhoda. **Carlton**.

Carlisle Old English: castle tower.
Carlyle.

Carlo Italian: a form of Charles.

Carlos Spanish and Portuguese: a
form of Charles.

Carlton English: transferred use of
a surname.

Carr Old Norse: from a marsh.

Carson Welsh: son of the marsh
dweller.

Carter Anglo-Saxon: cart maker.

Carver English: transferred use of
a surname.

Casey Irish: transferred use of a
surname. **Case**.

Cash a form of Caspar.

Caspar Persian: treasurer. **Casper**,
Cass, **Cash**, **Jasper**, **Gaspar**.

Cass Latin: proud of his appearance.

Cecil Latin: blind.

Cedric Celtic: war chief.

Chad Anglo-Saxon: fierce.

Chance a form of Chauncey.

Chandler Latin: candle maker.

Channing Irish: a little wolf cub.

Chanton English: transferred use of
a surname.

Chapin English: transferred use of
a surname.

Chapman English: peddler.

Charles German: strong, manly.
Charlie Chaplin, British-born silent film
star. **Charlie**, **Chip**, **Carl**, **Charlton**,
Chas, **Chaz**, **Carlos**, **Carlo**.

Charlton a form of Charles. Charlton
Heston, stage name of an American
actor.

Chas a form of Charles. Chaz
Palminteri, American actor. **Chaz**.

Chase Anglo-Norman: hunt.

Chauncey Latin: record-keeper.
Chance.

Cheney Old French: the oak wood. **Chaney**.

Chester Anglo-Saxon: camp-dweller. **Chet**.

Chevalier French: a knight.

Chevy Middle English: from the hunt. Chevy Chase, American actor.

Chip English: a form of Charles. **Chips, Chipper**.

Christian Latin: one who followed Christ. **Chris, Christie**.

Christo a form of Christopher.

Christophe French: a form of Christopher.

Christopher Greek: Christ-bearer. **Chris, Topher, Tiff, Christian, Christo, Christophe**.

Clancy Irish: a red warrior.

Clarence Latin: bright. Clarence Clemens, American musician. **Clare, Clary**.

Clark Anglo-Saxon: learned. Clark Kent, Superman's alter ego. **Clarke**.

Claude Latin: lame. **Claudio**.

Claus German: a form of Nicholas.

Clay English: he who lives in the clay fields.

Claybourne a form of Clayton.

Clayton Old English: settlement. **Clay, Claybourne**.

Clement Latin: merciful. **Clem, Clemence**.

Clifford Anglo-Saxon: cliff-dweller. **Cliff**.

Clifton Old English: from the cliff. **Cliff**.

Clint a form of Clinton. Clint Eastwood, American actor.

Clinton Anglo-Saxon: one who lives in a hill town. **Clint**.

Clive Anglo-Saxon: cliff-dweller. **Cleve**.

Clyde Celtic: one heard from a distance.

Cody Old English: a cushion.

Colbert French: mountain pass.

Cole English: swarthy one; a nickname for Nicholas.

Coleman Celtic: dove. **Colman**.

Colin Celtic: strong and victorious. **Collin**.

Colm Irish: a form of Colman.

Colman Irish: a form of the feminine name. **Columba**, **Colm**.

Colton English: from a coal town.

Conan Celtic: wise.

Connor Irish: lover of hounds. **Conor**.

Conrad Anglo-Saxon: bold. **Connie**, **Konrad**, **Cort**.

Constant English and French: steadfast.

Conway Welsh: from the holy river.

Cooper English: a barrel maker. **Kiefer**.

Corbett Latin: a raven.

Corbin Latin: raven-haired.

Cordell Old French: small rope. **Cord**.

Corey Celtic: dweller in a ravine. **Cory**.

Corin French: a spear.

Cornel a form of Cornelius. Cornel Wilde, American actor.

Cornelius Latin: hornlike. Cornelius Vanderbilt, American industrialist. **Cornel**, **Cornell**, **Neal**, **Neil**.

Cort English: a form of Conrad.

Cosmo Greek: crested like a lark.

Craig Celtic: mountain dweller.

Crane Old English: to stretch out.

Crispin Latin: curly-haired.

Crosby Anglo-Saxon: near a crossroad.

Cuddy Scottish: a form of Cuthbert; a donkey.

Cullen English: a holly tree.

Curran Irish: a champion.

Curtis Old French: courteous. Kurt Vonnegut, Jr., American author. **Curt**, **Kurt**.

Cuthbert Anglo-Saxon: brilliant. **Cuddy**.

Cyprien English and Latin: a man from Cyprus.

Cyril Greek: lordly. **Cyrille**.

Cyrus Persian: sun-like. **Ciro**, **Cy**.

Dabney Irish: transferred use of a surname.

Dacey Celtic: southern. **Dacy**.

Dacy a form of Dacey.

Dade English: transferred use of a surname.

Dagwood English: transferred use of a surname. Dagwood Bumstead, cartoon husband of Blondie; also, a sandwich.

Dakota Native American: a friend.

Dallas Scottish: from the waterfall.

Dale Anglo-Saxon: valley-dweller. **Dalton**.

Dalton a form of Dale.

Daly Celtic: counselor.

Damian Greek: a form of Damon.

Damiano Italian: a form of Damon.

Damon Greek: tame. **Damian, Damien, Damiano**.

Dan Anglo-Saxon: Danish. **Dane**.

Daniel Hebrew: the Lord is my judge. **Dan, Danny**.

Dante Italian: steadfast and enduring one.

Darby English and Irish: from Derby.

Darius Greek: wealthy king.

Darnell Old French: one who lurks in the secret place.

Darrell Old French: beloved. **Daryl**.

Darren Celtic: small but mighty.

Dashiell English: transferred use of a surname. Dashiell Hammett, American author. **Dash**.

David Hebrew: the beloved one. **Dave, Davey, Davy, Davis, Dovid**.

Davis a form of David.

Dawson English: a son of David.

Dean Anglo-Saxon: of the valley.

Declan Irish: a religious man.

Delaney Irish: a challenger's descendant.

Delano Irish: dark man.

Delmar Latin: of the sea. **Delmore**.

Delmore a form of Delmar.

Dempsey Greek: a lover of fine wines.

Denby Old Norse: from a Danish town.

Denis French: a form of Dionysus. **Dennis, Denny, Dennison**.

Dennison a form of Dennis.

Denver English: small valley.

Denzel Celtic: stronghold. Denzel Washington, American actor. **Denzil**.

Derek Anglo-Saxon: ruler. Derek Jeter, American baseball player. **Derrick**.

Dermot Celtic: who is free. **Dermott**.

Derry Celtic: red.

Desi Italian, Spanish, and Portuguese: a form of Desiderio. Desi Arnaz, Cuban bandleader and actor.

Desiderio Spanish: desired one. **Desi**.

Desmond Old English: of the south. Bishop Desmond Tutu, South African civil rights leader. **Des, Desi**.

Destry English: transferred use of a surname.

Devereux English: transferred use of a surname.

Devin Celtic: poet.

Devlin Celtic: brave one.

Dewey Old Welsh: beloved.

Dewitt English: transferred use of a surname.

Dexter Latin: fortunate. **Dex**.

Dick a form of Richard.

Dickie a form of Richard.

Dickson English: son of Dick. **Dicks, Dick, Dickie, Dicky, Dix**.

Didier French: longing for Christ.

Diego Spanish: a form of Jacob. Diego Rivera, Mexican artist.

Digby English: from the settlement. **Diggory**.

Diggory English: a form of Digby.

Dimitri Russian and Greek: a lover of the earth. **Dmitri, Dimitry**.

Dino Italian: short for names ending in "dino;" for example: Bernardino, Leonardino. Dino, nickname of American singer, Dean Martin.

Dinsmore Irish: castle on the hill.

Dion Greek: a form of Dionysus. Dion DiMucci, American musician.

Dionysus Greek: god of wine. **Dion, Denis**.

Dirk Flemish and Dutch: from Derek; also, Scottish: dagger. Dirk Bogarde, British actor.

Dix Anglo-Saxon: a form of Dickson and Dixon.

Dixon Anglo-Saxon: son of Dick. **Dix**.

Dobbin English: a form of Robert.

Dody English: pet form of the female name, Dorothy. **Dodie**.

Dolan Celtic: black-haired.

Dominic Latin: child born on the Lord's day. **Dom, Dominik, Nick**.

Donald Celtic: ruler. **Don, Donnel, Donnie**.

Donaldson Celtic: son of Donald.

Donovan Irish: deep brown. Donovan Leitch, Scottish singer.

Dorset English: from the name of a place.

Douglas Celtic: one who lives near the black water. Douglas Fairbanks, Jr., American actor. **Doug**, **Doogie**.

Dov Hebrew: bear.

Doyle Irish: variant of the name Dougal.

Drake English: a dragon.

Drew Anglo-Saxon: wise and honest.

Duane Irish: black.

Dudley Anglo-Saxon: from the meadow. Dudley Moore, British comedian and actor.

Duffy Scottish: dark one. **Duff**.

Duke Latin: leader.

Duncan Celtic: dark warrior.

Dunstan Anglo-Saxon: one who dwells near the brown stone hill.

Durand Latin: enduring one. **Dante**, **Durante**, **Durant**.

Durant a form of Durand.

Durwood Anglo-Saxon: guard. **Derwood**, **Durward**.

Dustin Old German: fighter. Dustin Hoffman, American actor. **Dusty**.

Dwight Anglo-Saxon: blond. Dwight David Eisenhower, 34th American president.

Dylan Old Welsh: from the sea. Dylan Thomas, Welsh poet.

Eamon Irish: a form of Edmund.

Earl Anglo-Saxon: warrior. James Earl Jones, American actor; Errol Flynn, Australian-born actor. **Earle, Errol.**

Easton a form of Eaton.

Eaton Anglo-Saxon: from the river. **Easton.**

Ebenezer Hebrew: rock of help. Ebenezer Scrooge, Dickens's protagonist in *A Christmas Carol*. **Eb.**

Edgar Anglo-Saxon: lucky warrior. Edgar Allan Poe, American author. **Ed, Eddie, Ned.**

Édouard a form of Edward.

Edmund Anglo-Saxon: happy and rich. Sir Edmund Hillary, New Zealand-born mountaineer. **Eamon.**

Edward Anglo-Saxon: prosperous guardian. **Ed, Eddie, Ned, Ted, Teddy, Edgar, Edmund, Edwin, Édouard.**

Edwin Anglo-Saxon: fortunate friend.

Egan Irish: fiery.

Egon German: edge of a sword. Egon Schiele, Austrian painter.

Eldon Teutonic: respected elder. **Eldin.**

Eldridge Old German: wise counselor.

Eleazer Hebrew: helped by God.

Eli Hebrew: highest. **Elian, Elias, Elijah, Elihu, Elly, Elio.**

Elian a form of Eli.

Elias Hebrew: the Lord is God; also, a form of Eli.

Elijah Hebrew: Yahweh is God. Elijah Wood, American actor. **Ellis.**

Ellery Teutonic: from the adler trees. Ellery Queen, fictional detective.

Elliot English: transferred use of a surname. Eliot Ness, American federal agent. **Eliot, Elliott.**

Ellis English: a form of Elijah.

Ellison Hebrew: son of Elias. **Elison.**

Elmer Anglo-Saxon: awe-inspiring. Elmer Fudd, befuddled cartoon character.

Elmo Greek: protector. Elmo, adorable Muppet.

Elroy Latin: royal king. Elroy Jetson, cartoon spaceboy. **Roy.**

Elton English: from the settlement. Elton John, stage name of British musician.

Elvin English: a form of Alvin.

Elvis English: transferred use of a surname; also, a 6th-century Irish saint. Elvis Presley, American musical legend.

Elwood Old English: of the old forest. Elwood Blues, legendary fictional musician, brother of Jake. **Ellwood.**

Emerson English: a form of Emery.

Emery Teutonic: ambitious leader. **Emory, Merrick, Emerson.**

Emil Teutonic: industrious. **Emile, Emilio.**

Emilio Italian, Spanish, and Portuguese: a form of Emil. Emilio Estevez, American actor.

Emlyn Teutonic: hard-working; also, Welsh: devotee.

Emmanuel Hebrew: God is with us. Emanuel Ax, Polish-born pianist. **Emanuel, Manuel.**

Emmet Teutonic: industrious saint. Emmett Kelly, American clown.

Emory a form of Emery.

Enoch Hebrew: dedicated; educated. **Eno**.

Enrico Italian: a form of Henry. Enrico Fermi, Italian physicist; Enrico Caruso, Italian tenor.

Enrique Spanish: a form of Henry.

Enzo Italian: a giant. Ezio Pinza, Italian opera singer. **Ezio**.

Ephraim Hebrew: fruitful. **Efram**, **Efrem**.

Eric Teutonic: kingly. **Erich**, **Erik**, **Rick**, **Ricky**.

Ernest Teutonic: sincere. **Ernst**, **Ernie**.

Esau Hebrew: twin of Jacob; hairy.

Esteban Spanish: a form of Steven. Esteban Cortazar, Columbian-born fashion designer.

Etan Hebrew: a form of Ethan.

Ethan Hebrew: strong. **Etan**.

Étienne French: a form of Steven.

Eugene Greek: noble. **Gene**.

Eustace English: of the grapes. A patron saint.

Evan Irish: well-born.

Everett Anglo-Saxon: strong and honored.

Ewan Welsh: a form of John. Ewan McGregor, Scottish actor. **Euan**.

Ezekiel Hebrew: my strength is my God. **Zeke**.

Ezra Hebrew: helpful one.

Fabian Latin: wealthy farmer. **Fabe**.

Fairfax Anglo-Saxon: fair-haired.

Fairfield English: from the name of a place.

Fallon Irish: from the name of a place.

Farleigh Old English: from the ram meadow. **Farley**.

Farquhar Old Celtic: dear man.

Farrell Celtic: brave one.

Felix Latin: lucky, happy one.

Felton Old Norse: from the hill town.

Fenton Old English: from the marshy settlement.

Ferdinand Latin: wild, bold, and courageous. **Ferdie, Fernando**.

Fergus Irish: strong.

Fernando Spanish and Portuguese: a form of Ferdinand. Fernando Lamas, Argentinian-born actor.

Field English: from the field. **Fields**.

Fields a form of Field.

Filmore English: from the name of a place.

Finbar Irish: fair-headed. **Finn**.

Finlay Scottish: fair warrior. **Finley**.

Finn Irish: fair and wise.

Fisher English: an occupational name; a fisherman.

Fitz English: short form of the surnames Fitzgerald and Fitzroy.

Fletcher Teutonic: arrowsmith. **Fletch**.

Flint Old English: a brook.

Florian German and Polish: a patron saint.

Flynn Irish: descendant of the red-haired man.

Ford English: one who lives near the river crossing.

Forest English: one who lives in the enclosed wood. Forest Whittaker, American actor. **Forrest**.

Foster English: forester; saddle-maker.

Fowler English: one who hunts wild fowl.

Francesco Italian: a form of the name Francis.

Francis Latin: free man; man from France. **Fran, Frank, Franck, François, Francesco, Franz, Paco**.

François French: from France.

Franklin Teutonic: landowner. Franklin Roosevelt, 32nd American president. **Frank, Frankie**.

Franz German: a form of Francis.

Fraser Scottish: transferred use of a surname. **Frasier**.

Fred a form of Alfred and Frederick.

Frederick Teutonic: peaceful ruler. **Frédérick, Fred, Freddy, Frederico, Rico, Fredo, Fritz**.

Freeman English: a free man. **Fremont**.

Fritz German: pet name for Friedrich.

Fulton Scottish: transferred use of surname.

Gabriel Hebrew: strong man of God. Gabriel Byrne, Irish actor. **Gabe, Barie.**

Gage Old French: a pledge.

Gaines Old French: one who increases in wealth and prestige.

Galen Greek: wise healer.

Gannon English: one who is fair-skinned.

Gardiner Teutonic: gardener.

Gareth Welsh: gentle one.

Garfield English: one who lives near the triangular field.

Garner Teutonic: gardener.

Garrett Old English: mighty spear. **Garret, Gareth, Gary, Garth, Gerard, Jaret.**

Garrick Teutonic: great warrior. **Arick, Rick, Ricky.**

Garrison French: from the fortified place.

Garson English: son of Garth.

Garth Welsh: one who lives near an enclosure or garden.

Garvey a form of Garvin.

Garvin Irish: little, rough one. **Garvan,
Garvey**.

Gary Old English: spear thrower.

Gaspar Hungarian: a form of Caspar.
Jasper.

Gaston French: a guest.

Gautier French: a form of Walter.

Gavin Old Welsh: of the hawk field.

Gaylord French: high-spirited.

Gaynor Irish: son of a fair-skinned
man.

Gene a form of Eugene.

Geoffrey Teutonic: God's peace
throughout the land. **Geoff, Jeff,
Jeffers, Jeffrey, Godfrey**.

Geordie Scottish: a form of George.

George Greek: farmer. George
Washington, 1st American president.
**Georges, Georgie, Geordie, Jorge,
Jurgen**.

Gerald Teutonic: spearman. Gerald
Ford, 38th American president.
Jerrold, Gerry, Jerry, Jerome.

Gerard English: strong spear. **Gerry,
Gerhard, Gerrit**.

Gerhard a form of Gerard.

Gerrit a form of Gerard.

Gerry German: a form of Gerard
and Gerald.

Giacomo Italian: a form of James.

Gian Italian: a form of John.

Giancarlo Italian: a form of John and
Carl.

Gianni Italian: a form of John.

Gibson Hebrew: strong.

Gideon Hebrew: feller of trees.

Gifford Teutonic: generous gift. **Gif**.

Gil Spanish Portuguese: a form
of Giles.

Gilbert Teutonic: brilliant promise. Gilbert Gottfried, American comedian. **Gil, Gib, Bert.**

Giles Greek: goat. **Gilles, Gil.**

Gilmore Old Norse: from the deep glen.

Gilroy Irish: son of a red-haired lad.

Gino Italian: short form of names ending in "gino."

Giovanni Italian: a form of John.

Giverny French: from the name of a place.

Glendon a form of Glenn.

Glenford a form of Glenn.

Glenn Celtic: valley-dweller. Glenn Ford, Canadian-born actor. **Glen, Glendon, Glenford.**

Goddard a form of Godwin.

Godfrey Norman: good and peaceful.

Godwin Old English: good friend. **Goodwin, Goddard.**

Gordon Celtic: hill. Gordon Lightfoot, Canadian-born musician. **Gordie, Gordy.**

Grady Irish: noble one.

Graham Old English: of the gray place. Graham Greene, British author. **Gram, Bram, Ham.**

Grant Middle English: one who is great.

Granville Old French: from the old settlement.

Gray Old English: gray-haired. **Grey.**

Graydon English: transferred use of a surname.

Grayson English: son of the bailiff.

Grégoire French: a form of Gregory.

Gregory Greek: watchman. Gregory Peck, American actor. **Greg, Grégoire.**

Griffin Welsh: a form of Griffith. Griffin Dunne, American actor.

Gunnar Scandinavian: a form of Gunther. Gunnar Nelson, American musician.

Gunther Teutonic: brave fighter.

Gus Scottish: a form of Gustave, Angus, and Augustus.

Gustave Scandinavian: staff of the nobles. Gustave Flaubert, French author; Gustave Courbet, French painter. **Gus**.

Guy Teutonic: leader. Guy de Maupassant, pen name of French author. **Guido**.

Griffith Celtic: strong chief; red-haired. **Griff, Griffin, Rufus**.

Griswold Old German: from the gray forest.

Grosvenor French: a large hunter.

Grover Old English: one who lives near the grove of trees. Grover Cleveland, 22nd and 24th American president.

Guido Italian: a form of Guy.

Guillaume French: a form of William.

h

Hadden Anglo-Saxon: from the valley of the heath. **Haddan, Haddon, Haden, Hayden.**

Haden a form of Hadden.

Hadrian Latin: a dark one.

Hagen Celtic: little. **Hagan.**

Haines Anglo-Saxon: a vine-covered cottage. **Haynes.**

Halden Teutonic: half-Danish man. **Haldan, Haldin.**

Hale Teutonic: robust. **Hal.**

Halsey Anglo-Saxon: from Hal's island. **Halsy.**

Halstead Anglo-Saxon: from the manor house.

Hamilton Anglo-Saxon: one who loves his home; also, French: he is from the mountain. Hamilton Fish, American diplomat. **Ham.**

Hamish Hebrew: may God protect him. Hamish Bowles, British fashion expert.

Hamlin German: he who loves a small home.

Hans Hebrew: gift of Jehovah; also, German: a form of John.

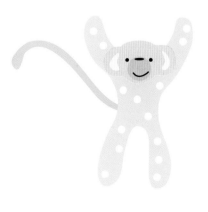

Hansen Scandinavian: son of Hans; son of John. **Hanson.**

Harcourt Teutonic: courtyard of the soldiers.

Harden Anglo-Saxon: like a hare.

Harding Anglo-Saxon: son of the brave one.

Hardy German: courageous one.

Harlan Old English: place of the hares. **Harland.**

Harley Anglo-Saxon: meadow of the hares. **Arlie, Harleigh.**

Hartley Old English: from the stag woods.

Harlow Anglo-Saxon: the protected hill.

Harmon Greek: to join together.

Harold Norse: great and powerful warrior. Harold Pinter, British writer. **Hal, Harald, Harry, Herold.**

Harper Anglo-Saxon: harp player. Harpo Marx, stage name of American comedian. **Harpo.**

Harrington English: from the name of a place.

Harris a form of Harrison.

Harrison Teutonic: son of Harry. **Harris, Harry.**

Harry a familiar form of Henry and Harrison. Harry Houdini, stage name of Hungarian-born escape artist.

Hart German: a stag.

Harvey German: he who protects his homeland; also, French: bitter. **Harv, Hervey, Hervé, Javier.**

Haydon Teutonic: he who is from the enclosed valley. **Hayden.**

Hayes Anglo-Saxon: hunter.

Heath Anglo-Saxon: from the wasteland.

Heathcliff Anglo-Saxon: from the cliff of the wasteland.

Hector Greek: steadfast defender. Hector Elizondo, American actor.

Henri French: a form of Henry.

Henry German: ruler of the home or estate. **Hal, Hank, Harry, Henri, Enrico, Enrique.**

Herbert Teutonic: bright warrior. Herbert Hoover, 31st American president. **Bert, Herb, Herbie.**

Herman Teutonic: bright warrior.

Herschel Hebrew: deer. Herschel Bernardi, American actor. **Hershel, Hersh**.

Hervé French: a form of Harvey.

Hewitt French and German: little Hugh.

Hilliard Teutonic: war guardian.

Hilton Anglo-Saxon: from the estate of hills.

Hiram Hebrew: exalted and noble one; moral. **Hi, Hy**.

Hiroshi Japanese: generous one.

Hitchcock English: transferred use of a surname. **Hitch**.

Hobart Teutonic: bright and intelligent one. **Bart, Hobbie, Hobie**.

Hogan Irish: young one.

Holden Anglo-Saxon: gentle one.

Hollis Anglo-Saxon: he who dwells in the holly tree grove. **Holl, Holly**.

Homer Greek: pledge or security.

Holt Old English: son of the unspoiled forests.

Horace Latin: he who marks time. Horace Mann, American educator.

Horatio Latin: transferred use of a clan name. Horatio Alger, American writer. **Horacio, Horry, Race**.

Houston English: a hill town.

Howard Teutonic: guardian and protector.

Hubbel English: transferred use of a surname.

Hubert Teutonic: genius. Hubert Humphrey, American politician. **Bert, Hube, Hubie, Huberto, Hugh**.

Hudson English: a form of Hugh.

Hugh Norman: heart, mind, spirit. Hugh Grant, British actor. **Hughie, Huey, Hugo, Hudson**.

Hugo Latin: a form of Hugh.

Humphrey Teutonic: guardian of peace. Humphrey Bogart, American actor.

Hunter English: a hunter. Hunter S. Thompson, American author. **Hunt**.

Ian Irish: gracious is the Lord. Ian Fleming, British author and creator of James Bond.

Igor Scandinavian: hero. Igor Stravinsky, Russian composer.

Inigo English: from Spanish, Ignatius. Inigo Jones, 17th-century British architect.

Irvin a form of Irving.

Irving Old English: protector of the oceans. **Erwin, Irwin, Irvine, Irvin.**

Irwin a form of Irving.

Isaac Hebrew: born with humor. Sir Isaac Newton, 17th-century mathematician. **Isaak, Izaak, Ike, Izzy, Itch.**

Isaiah Hebrew: help comes from God. Isaiah Thomas, American basketball player. **Isaia.**

Isidore Greek: a gift. **Dorian, Dore, Dory, Izzy, Issy, Isador.**

Israel Hebrew: the one with whom God rules. **Izzy.**

Ivan Russian: gift from God. **Vanya.**

Ivar Scandinavian: master of bow and arrow. **Iver, Ives, Ivor, Yves.**

j

Jack Middle English: God's gift. **Jackie, Jake, Jock, Jocko.**

Jackie a form of Jack. Jackie Mason, American comedian.

Jackson English: the son of Jack. Jackson Pollock, American painter; Jackson Browne, American musician.

Jacob Hebrew: one who takes the place of another; Esau's twin. **Jake, Jakie, Jakob, Yakov, Jock, Jacques, Diego, Koby.**

Jacques French: a form of Jacob. Jacques Cousteau, French environmentalist and undersea explorer. **Jack, Jock.**

Jaden Hebrew: God has heard.

Jake a form of Jacob.

Jamal Arabic: handsome. Malcolm-Jamal Warner, American actor. **Jamar.**

James Hebrew: he who succeeds another. **Jamie, Jimmy, Jameson, Jaime, Jaimie, Jim, Seamus, Jem, Jemmie, Giacomo.**

Jameson a form of James.

Jared Hebrew: of good fortune, long life. **Jarret, Jarrod.**

Jarret a form of Jared.

Jarrod a form of Jared.

Jarvis English: skilled with a spear. **Jervis, Gervais.**

Jason Greek: has capacity to heal. **Jace.**

Jasper Persian: bright gem. **Casper, Kasper, Kass.**

Javier Spanish: a form of Harvey. Javier Bardem, Spanish actor.

Jay Anglo-Saxon: bird; energetic.

Jean French: a form of John.

Jeb a form of Jedidiah.

Jed a form of Jedidiah.

Jedidiah Hebrew: friend of God. **Jed, Jeb.**

Jefferson Teutonic: unconflicted. **Jeff, Jeffrey, Jeffery, Geoffrey, Jeffy.**

Jeffrey a form of Jefferson. **Jeff.**

Jens Scandinavian: a form of John.

Jeremiah Hebrew: he who is empowered by God. **Jeremy.**

Jeremy English: a form of Jeremiah. **Jeremias, Jerry, Jeron.**

Jermaine English: a form of Germany.

Jerome a form of Gerald. Jerome Kern, American songwriter.

Jeron a form of Jeremy.

Jerry a form of Gerald or Gerard. Jerry Seinfeld, American comedian.

Jervis a form of Jarvis.

Jesse Hebrew: fortune; gift from God. Jesse James, American outlaw. **Jess, Jessie.**

Jesus Spanish and Portuguese: celebrating Christ's name; savior. **Chus, Chucho.**

Jethro Hebrew: exceptional, superior. Jethro Bodine, one of television's *Beverly Hillbillies*; and Jethro Tull, American rock group. **Jeth.**

Joaquin Spanish and Hebrew: judgment; from God. **Joachim, Joacquin.**

Jobie Hebrew: paternity. **Joab.**

Jock a form of Jacob.

Jody English: possible variant of Jude; male and female name. **Jude, Jodie.**

Joel Hebrew: commanding one; also, a form of Joseph. Joel Grey, American actor.

Johan a form of John.

Johannes a form of John. Johann Sebastian Bach, 18th-century German composer.

John Hebrew: graciousness of God; the Lord's gift. John Fitzgerald Kennedy, 35th American president. **Jon, Johnny, Johan, Johann, Johannes, Hans, Juan, Gian, Gianni, Giovanni, Jevon, Jan, Jens, Jean, Shane, Sean, Shaun, Shawn, Zane, Nino, Ewan, Euan.**

Jon a form of Jonathan.

Jonah Hebrew: sign of peace. **Jonas, Jone, Jones, Yonah.**

Jonas a form of Jonah. American physician Jonas Salk discovered the polio vaccine.

Jonathan Hebrew: graciousness. **Jon.**

Jones a form of Jonah.

Jordan English and German: from the river Jordan; to flow like a river. **Jordie, Giordano, Jourdain.**

Jordie a form of Jordan.

José a form of Joseph.

Joseph Hebrew: he who adds and increases. Joseph Cornell, American artist. **Joe, Joey, Jojo, Jody, Joel, José, Yossi.**

Josh a form of Joshua.

Joshua Hebrew: God is the savior. **Josh, Jozua, Giosue.**

Josiah Hebrew: supportive is God. **Josie, Joss.**

Juan a form of John.

Judah Hebrew: the Lord's praise. **Jude, Judas, Judd, Jud, Judson.**

Judd a form of Judah.

Judson a form of Judah.

Julio Spanish: a form of Julius. Julio Iglesias, Spanish singer.

Julius Latin: immortal spirit, young at heart. **Jules, Jule, Juley, Julian, Julien, Julio.**

Junior Latin: young.

Justin Latin: of virtue; upstanding. **Justis, Justus.**

Kai Scandinavian: rooster. **Kay, Kaj, Cayo, Kajik.**

Kalman Hungarian: a pilgrim who made miracles after his death. **Colman.**

Kane Irish: rebel; with fiery spirit. **Cathan.**

Karsten Greek: anointed one.

Kaspar Persian: a treasurer; also, German and Scandinavian: a form of Caspar. **Caspar, Casper, Kass, Jaspar.**

Keaton English: from an estate.

Keddy Scottish: a form of Adam.

Keegan Irish: fiery, little one.

Keenan Irish: ancient little one.

Keir Celtic: swarthy. **Kerr.**

Keirnan a form of Kieran.

Keith Irish: soldier; also, English and Scottish: from wood.

Kelby Old German: from a farm by the spring. **Kelbie.**

Kelly Irish: courageous soldier. Often used as a feminine name. **Kelley, Kellie.**

Kendall Celtic: lord of the valley; of the river Kent; spring. **Kendale, Kendal.**

Kendrick English and Old Celtic: revered; mountain-top.

Kennedy Anglo-Saxon; from Irish: leader, intimidating.

Kenneth Celtic: handsome, good looks. **Ken, Kenny, Kent.**

Kent a form of Kenneth.

Kenyon Celtic: fair-haired one. **Ken, Kenny.**

Kermit Celtic: free to be. **Dermot, Kerry.**

Kern Irish: a form of Kieran.

Kerwin Irish: black-haired little one.

Kes English: from the word "kestrel," a falcon.

Kevin Celtic: kind, handsome, lovable. Kevin Kline, American actor. **Kev, Keven.**

Kiefer German: a form of Cooper. **Keifer.**

Kieran Irish: black. **Keirnan, Ciaran, Kyran, Kern.**

Kimball Anglo-Saxon: commander, bold one. **Kemble, Kim, Kimble.**

King English: having royal, kingly qualities. **Kingley.**

Kip Old English: a pointed hill. **Kipp, Kippie, Kippy.**

Kirby Teutonic: church town dweller. **Kerby, Kerr.**

Kirk Scandinavian: resides close to a church.

Knightly Old English: a knight.

Knowles Old English: a grassy hill.

Knox Old English: from the hill.

Koby Hungarian: from the name Jacob.

Kurt a form of Curtis.

Kyle Irish: narrow; handsome one. Kyle MacLachlan, American actor.

Lachlan Scottish Gaelic: spirited fighter. **Lachann, Lockie.**

Laddie Old English: young servant. **Ladd.**

Lafayette Old French: faithful. French statesman, general, and hero of the American Revolution.

Lakeland English: lake.

Lamar Teutonic: famous one.

Lambert Teutonic: owning much land; bright. **Lambert, Bertie, Bert.**

Lance Anglo-Saxon: sword, land. Lance Armstrong, American bicycling champion. **Lancelot, Lancey, Launce.**

Landis a form of Landry.

Landon a form of Langston.

Landry French: a ruler. **Landis, Lansing.**

Langdon a form of Langston.

Langston Anglo-Saxon: one respected for his position. Langston Hughes, American poet. **Landon, Langdon, Langley.**

Lansing a form of Landry.

Laramie French: he who comes from Aramis.

Lars Scandinavian: crowned with laurel; successful. **Larson**.

Latham Old English: landowner.

Latimer Anglo-Saxon: translator, interpreter, teacher.

Laughlin Irish: of Lochlainn.

Laurent a form of Lawrence.

Lawrence Latin: honored with laurel wreaths. Sir Laurence Olivier, British actor. **Laurence, Larry, Laurent, Laurie, Lauren, Loren, Lorenzo**.

Lee Anglo-Saxon: of the meadow. **Leigh, Leland**.

Leif Scandinavian: beloved. **Leaf**.

Leighton English: of a leek meadow. **Layton**.

Lemuel Hebrew: dedicated. **Lem, Lemmie, Lemmy**.

Lenon Irish: cape. **Lennon**.

Leo Latin: bold like a lion. **Leon, Lionel, Lyonel**.

Leon a form of Leo.

Leonard Teutonic: courageous with lions. Leonard Cohen, Canadian singer-songwriter. **Len, Lenny, Lennie**.

Leroy Old French: king. **Elroy, Leroi, Rex, Roy, Lee**.

Lester Latin: from a favored military corps. **Les**.

Lev Russian: like a lion. **Lyov, Leib, Liev**.

Levi Hebrew: of another; related.

Lewis Teutonic: honored fighter. **Clovis, Louis, Louie, Lew, Lewes, Ludorick**.

Liam a form of William. Liam Neeson, Irish actor.

Lincoln English: of the lake region; associated with Abraham Lincoln, 16th American president. **Lin, Linc, Link**.

Lindsey Old English: of the ornamental Linden tree. **Lindsay, Lindsy**.

Linus Greek: boy with hair of gold. Linus Pauling, American scientist.

Lionel Old French: brave like a young lion. Lionel Barrymore, American actor. **Leo**.

Lloyd Welsh: dark-skinned, gray one. **Floyd.**

Lodge Old French: cottage.

Logan Irish: of a small valley.

London English: fortress. **Lonnie.**

Lonnie Irish: little, yet strong. **Lon.**

Lorcan Irish: aggressive one.

Lord Old English: head of the household.

Loren a form of Lawrence.

Lorenzo a form of Lawrence. Lorenzo de Medici, 15th-century Florentine ruler and patron of the arts.

Lorne English and Canadian: from the land of Lorne in Argyll. Lorne Greene, American actor.

Louis a form of Lewis. **Aloysisus.**

Lowell Anglo-Saxon: loved, adored one. Lowell Thomas, American writer and broadcast journalist.

Lucas Latin: one who introduces knowledge and energy. **Luke, Luc, Luka, Lucais.**

Lucien a form of Lucius.

Lucius Latin: child of the dawn. **Lucien, Lucian.**

Lucky English: good fortune.

Luke a form of Lucas.

Luther Teutonic: brave one. **Lothair, Lothar, Lothario.**

Lyle Old French: of the isle.

Lyndon Old English: residing near linden trees. Lyndon Johnson, 36th American president. **Lin, Lindon.**

Mac Irish: son.

Mackenzie Irish: son of a fair-haired man.

Magnus Latin: great one.

Maine Native American: a state.

Major Latin: champion.

Malachi Hebrew: messenger of God.

Malcolm Scotch Irish: one who follows St. Columbia.

Malik Arabic: master.

Marc French: a form of Mark.

Marcel Latin: belongs to the god Mars. **Marcello, Marcellus**.

Marco Italian: a form of Mark.

Mario Latin: a child of Mars; bitter or rebellious. Mario Lanza, legendary American tenor.

Mark Latin: a warrior; a child of Mars. **Marc, Marky, Markie, Marcus, Marco, Marx**.

Marley Anglo-Saxon: of the lake meadow.

Marlon a form of Merlin. Marlon Brando, American actor; Marlon Wayans, American comedian.

Marshall Old French: officer who commands horses; a warden or marshal. Marshall Field, American entrepreneur.

Marston Anglo-Saxon: from the marsh. **Marsden, Denny.**

Martin Latin: warlike; child of the god Mars. Martin Luther King, Jr., American civil rights leader. **Marty.**

Marvin Teutonic: renowned; one who is a friend of the ocean. **Mervin, Merwyn.**

Marx German: a form of Mark. Karl Marx, German politician, philosopher, and founder of socialism.

Maslin Old French: little twin.

Mason French: stone builder.

Matteo Italian and Spanish: a form of Matthew.

Matthew Hebrew: a benevolent gift from the Lord. Matthew Broderick, American actor. **Matt, Mattie, Matty, Matthieu, Matteo.**

Maurice Latin: one with black hair. **Maury, Mauricio, Maruizio**.

Max Latin: greatest one; superior. **Maxwell, Maximilian, Maxie, Maxim**.

Mayer a form of Meyer. Nathan Mayer Rothschild, 19th-century German financier.

Maynard Teutonic: commanding man; potency; firmness. Maynard G. Krebs, beatnik friend of television's Dobie Gillis.

Meade Anglo-Saxon: one from the meadow.

Melvin Celtic: refined leader. **Mel**.

Mercer Middle English: one who deals in expensive textiles. Mercer Mayer, American author; Merce Cunningham, American choreographer. **Merce**.

Merle French: blackbird; dark-haired child.

Merlin Welsh: from the fort by the sea; Latin: a falcon. Arthurian wizard. **Marlon**.

Merrill Old French: small and famous.

Mervin a form of Marvin.

Merwyn a form of Marvin.

Meyer Teutonic: assistant to a king; a steward. **Mayer**.

Micah Hebrew: like unto Jehovah; observing.

Michael Hebrew: one who is like God; worthy. **Mike, Mikie, Mick, Micky, Mickey, Micah, Michel, Mischa, Mitchell**.

Mickey a form of Michael. Mickey Mouse, Disney cartoon character. **Mick**.

Miles Latin: a warrior. Miles Davis, American jazz trumpet player. **Myles**.

Milford English: from the mill by the ford.

Millard Anglo-Saxon: flatterer. Millard Fillmore, 13th American president.

Miller English: one who grinds the grain.

Millis English: transferred use of a place name.

Mills English: from the mill.

Milo Latin: a warrior; a merciful donor.

Milson English: son of the miller.

Milton Anglo-Saxon: one who is from a milling town or home. John Milton, 17th-century British poet.

Mischa Russian: a form of Michael. **Mish**.

Mitchell a form of Michael. **Mitch**.

Mohammed Arabic: deserving of praise; one who has exceptional character. Muhammad, founder and Prophet of Islam. **Muhammad**.

Monroe Celtic: one who is from the red bog.

Montague Latin: of the mountain. **Monty**.

Montana Native American: a state.

Montgomery French: from the castle on the mountain. **Monty**.

Moore Celtic: from the moors.

Moran English: transferred use of a surname.

Mordechai Hebrew: Esther's cousin and foster father. **Mordy**.

Morgan Welsh: a dazzling ocean dweller; born by the ocean.

Morley Anglo-Saxon: a field of ferns.

Morris Latin: dark-skinned; a Berber. **Maury**.

Morrison English: son of Morris.

Mortimer Latin: quiet and tranquil like water; soldier of the sea. **Morty, Mort**.

Morton Old English: home by a marsh or bog. **Morty, Mort**.

Moses Hebrew: child rescued from the water. **Moises, Moss**.

Moss a form of Moses.

Murdoch Celtic: a rich protector of the ocean.

Murphy Celtic: transferred use of a surname.

Murray Celtic: a mariner; happy.

Myron Greek: perfumed or sweet oil.

Napoleon Teutonic: son of the mist. Napoleon Bonaparte, 19th-century Emperor of France.

Nash English: transferred use of a surname.

Natale Latin: day of birth.

Nathan Hebrew: given by the Lord. Nathan Hale, hero of the American Revolution. **Nat, Natan**.

Nathaniel Hebrew: a present from the Lord God. Nathaniel Hawthorne, 19th-century American writer. **Nate**.

Neal a form of Neil. **Niles, Nils**.

Ned a form of Edward.

Neil Irish: noted soldier; victor; champion. **Neal, Niles, Nils**.

Nelson Celtic: the offspring of Neal. **Nels**.

Nestor Greek: homecoming.

Neville Norman: transferred use of a surname. Arthur Neville Chamberlain, British prime minister.

Nevin Irish: one who worships; also, Old German: nephew. **Nevan**.

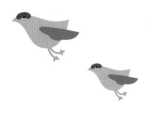

Nicholas Greek: triumphant people; conquerors. Nicholas Romanov, the last Tsar of Russia. **Nick, Nicky, Nico, Nicolas, Claus.**

Nigel Latin: one from Nigellas; dark-skinned.

Niles a form of Neal.

Nils a form of Neal. Nils Lofgren, American musician.

Nino a form of John.

Noah Hebrew: soothe; to rest after traveling. Noah Webster, American lexicographer.

Noble Latin: well-born.

Noel Latin: Christmas day. Noel Coward, British playwright.

Nolan Irish: chariot fighter; victor. Nolan Ryan, American baseball player.

Norbert Teutonic: a brilliant and celebrated person from the north. **Norbie.**

Norman Anglo-Saxon: a man from the north. Norman Mailer, American playwright.

North Middle English: the direction of the north terrestrial pole.

Norton Anglo-Saxon: from the northern lands. Norton Simon, American art collector and businessman.

Oakes Middle English: a tree from the beech family that produces acorns.

Oakley Anglo-Saxon: of the field of oak trees.

Ocean Middle English: the whole body of salt water that covers three-quarters of the earth.

Odell Teutonic: one who is prosperous; affluent. **Odie, Odin**.

Ogden Anglo-Saxon: from the dale of the oaks. Ogden Nash, American humorist poet.

Olaf Old Norse: relic, forebear; reminder of harmony and accord.

Oliver Latin: olive tree; a sign of peace; one who is generous. Oliver Platt, Canadian actor. **Olivier, Ollie**.

Omar Arabic: the greatest; first-born son; celestial; opulence. Omar Sharif, Egyptian-born actor.

Oren Hebrew: pine. **Orrin**.

Ori Middle English: porch. **Oriel**.

Orlando a form of Roland. Orlando Bloom, British actor.

Orleans French: a town in north central France.

183

Orson Latin: a man like a bear. Orson Wells, American actor.

Orville Anglo-Saxon: one who is the sword companion. Orville Wright, pioneer American aviator. **Orvin**.

Osbourne Anglo-Saxon: perfectly brilliant; vivid. Ozzy Osbourne, British musician. **Ozzie**, **Ozzy**.

Oscar Anglo-Saxon: faultless spear; spear man. Oscar Wilde, Irish writer.

Osgood Old English: he is divinely good.

Oswald Anglo-Saxon: god-like strength; godly force. **Ozzie**.

Otis Greek: one who has sharp hearing. Otis Redding, American musician.

Otto Teutonic: rich; well-to-do; affluent. Prince Otto von Bismarck, German statesman.

Owen Celtic: youthful soldier of noble birth. Jesse Owen, American Olympic athlete.

p

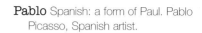

Pablo Spanish: a form of Paul. Pablo Picasso, Spanish artist.

Paco a form of Francis. Paco Rabanne, Spanish fashion designer.

Paine Latin: a person from the country; rural; down-to-earth. **Payne**.

Palmer Latin: a palm-carrying pilgrim.

Parker English: a park keeper.

Parnell Old French: small; a form of Peter.

Pascal Latin: relating to Easter. **Pasquale**.

Patrick Latin: honest; noble; patrician. Patrick Ewing, Jamaican-born basketball player. **Pat**.

Paul Latin: small. Paul Revere, 18th-century American silversmith and patriot. **Paulie, Pablo, Paolo, Pavel**.

Pavel Spanish: a form of Paul.

Paxton Old English: from the peaceful town.

Payson English: transferred use of a surname.

Payton a form of Peyton.

Pedro Spanish: a form of Peter.

Pembroke Welsh: an area in southwest Wales.

Penn English: transferred use of a surname. William Penn founded the state of Pennsylvania.

Percival Old French: one who pierces the valley. **Percy.**

Percy a form of Percival.

Peregrine English: foreigner; outsider.

Perry Anglo-Saxon: a pear tree; any tree that grows fruit.

Peter Greek: rock; stone. **Pete, Peterson, Pierre, Pedro, Pierce, Piers, Parnell.**

Peterson Greek: Peter's son.

Peyton Old English: from the fighter's estate. **Payton.**

Phelan Irish: wolf.

Phelps English: son of Philip.

Philip Greek: one who loves horses. **Phillip, Philippe, Phipps, Pip.**

Phineas Egyptian: a person of Nubian descent. **Finn.**

Phipps a form of Philip.

Pierce a form of Peter. Pierce Brosnan, Irish actor.

Pierre a form of Peter.

Piers a form of Peter.

Pierson Middle English: Peter's son.

Pip a form of Philip.

Platt German: flat; low.

Polls Middle English: the nape of the neck.

Porter Middle English: a gatekeeper.

Portland English: transferred use of a surname.

Powell Old Welsh: progeny of Howell.

Prentice Middle English: novice; one who is learning.

Prescott Old English: priest's cottage.

Presley English: a priest's meadow. Elvis Presley, American musician.

Preston Anglo-Saxon: from the place of the holy one.

Prewitt French: little and brave.

Price Middle English: assessment; worth.

Prosper Latin: fortunate; successful.

Putnam Old English: he who lives by the pond.

Quentin Latin: the fifth child. Quentin Tarantino, American actor and filmmaker. **Quinton**.

Quincy Irish: living at the house of the fifth son. John Quincy Adams, 6th American president.

Quinlan Irish: strong one.

Quinn Irish: possessing wisdom and intelligence.

Quinton a form of Quentin.

Rain Middle English: a fall of water dropping from the sky.

Ralph Teutonic: a wolf who is swift and nimble. Ralph Fiennes, British actor. **Rafe**, **Rolf**.

Ramsey Anglo-Saxon: a fierce, powerful island; wooded island. **Ramsay**.

Rand a form of Randolph.

Randall a form of Randolph.

Randolph Saxon: wolf shield. William Randolph Hearst, American newspaper mogul. **Randy**, **Randall**, **Rand**.

Ranger British: one who enforces the law over a wide area of land.

Raoul a form of Rudolph. Raul Julia, Puerto Rican-born actor. **Raul**.

Raphael Hebrew: healed by God. Raphael, 16th-century Italian Renaissance painter. **Rafi**, **Rafael**.

Raymond Teutonic: sage protector; recommended defense. Raymond Yard, American jeweler. **Ray**, **Ramon**.

Rémy French: one who rows a boat.

Redmond Old English: one who advises and defends.

Reece Welsh: passion; zeal. **Reese.**

Reed Middle English: a tall grass; arrow.

Reeve Middle English: a bailiff.

Regan Irish: a young person with a noble title; young monarch.

Reginald Saxon: potent; powerful; strong. **Reggie, Reg, Reynaldo, Reynolds.**

Rembrandt Dutch: surname of a 17th-century painter.

René French: revitalized; reborn.

Reno Native American: a city in Nevada.

Reuben Hebrew: a son is born. Ruben Blades, Panamanian-born actor and singer. **Ruby, Ruben, Reuven.**

Reuven a form of Reuben. **Ruby.**

Rex Latin: king. Rex Harrison, British actor.

Reynaldo a form of Reginald.

Reynard Teutonic: strong; a fox.

Reynolds a form of Reginald.

Rhett Welsh: fervent. Rhett Butler, fictional hero in *Gone with the Wind*.

Richard Teutonic: powerful leader; prosperous. **Rich, Richie, Rick, Ricky, Rico, Ricardo, Dick, Dickie.**

Richmond Teutonic: powerful custodian; defender of the poor.

Rico a form of Frederick.

Rider Middle English: one who travels on the back of an animal. **Ryder, Ry.**

Ridley Old English: one who comes from a red field. Ridley Scott, British filmmaker.

Riley Irish: brave.

Ring Old English: ring. **Ringo.**

Ringo a form of Ring. Ringo Starr, British musician.

Rip Dutch: developed; ripe. Rip Torn, American actor.

Ripley Anglo-Saxon: from the field of one who yells.

River Middle English: a river. River Phoenix, American actor.

Roarke Irish: celebrated ruler. Howard Roarke, protagonist in Ayn Rand's *The Fountainhead*.

Robert Teutonic: brilliant eminence. Robert was the name of two dukes of Normandy, including the father of William the Conqueror. **Rob**, **Robbie**, **Robby**, **Bob**, **Bobby**, **Robin**, **Dobbin**, **Robinson**, **Rupert**.

Robin a form of Robert. Robin Williams, American comedian and actor.

Robinson a form of Robert. Robinson Crusoe, fictional character by Daniel Defoe.

Rocco a form of Rochester. **Rock**, **Rocky**.

Rochester Old English: rocky fortress. Rochester, Jack Benny's fictional radio butler. **Chet**, **Rocco**.

Rockwell Old English: from the rocky watering hole.

Rocky a form of Rocco.

Rod Teutonic: well-known lord; illustrious. Rod Stewart, British singer. **Roddy**, **Roderick**, **Roderic**.

Roderick a form of Rod. **Roderic**.

Rodman Teutonic: memorable person; brave; redheaded; a knight's helper.

Rodney Teutonic: notorious. Rodney Dangerfield, American comedian.

Roger Teutonic: one who is known for his lancing abilities. Roger Moore, British actor.

Rohan Irish: red.

Roland Teutonic: from the illustrious place. **Orlando**, **Rollo**, **Rolly**, **Rowley**.

Rolf a form of Rudolph.

Rollo a form of Roland.

Roman Russian: a person from Rome.

Romeo Italian: one who journeys to Rome; notoriety. Shakespearean character, Romeo Montague, Juliet Capulet's lover.

Ronald Old Norse: commanding authority. **Ron**, **Ronnie**.

Ronan Irish: the ocean seal. Dr. Ronan Tynan, Irish tenor.

Roone a form of Rooney.

Rooney Irish: red-haired. **Roone**.

Roosevelt North American: Theodore and Franklin Delano Roosevelt, the 26th and the 32nd American presidents.

Rory Celtic: red. Rory Calhoun, American actor.

Roscoe Old Norse: from the forest where the deer live.

Ross Teutonic: horse; peninsula; red.

Rourke English: transferred use of a surname.

Rowan English: small red one.

Rowley English: wild, unruly forest.

Roy Latin: king; also, Celtic: redheaded.

Royce Old English: prince.

Rudolph Teutonic: legendary wolf. Rudolph Valentino, Italian-born actor. **Rudy, Raul, Raoul, Rolf**.

Rudy a form of Rudolph.

Rudyard Teutonic: prominence; also, Old English: from the red enclosure. Rudyard Kipling, Indian-born British writer.

Rufus Latin: redheaded.

Rupert a form of Robert.

Rush a form of Russell.

Russ a form of Russell.

Russell Latin: redheaded or Anglo-Saxon: like a fox. **Russ, Rusty, Rush**.

Rusty a form of Russell.

Rutherford Anglo-Saxon: from the stream where the cattle drink. Rutherford B. Hayes, 19th American president. **Ford**.

Ryan Irish: prince. Ryan O'Neal, American actor.

Ryder English: a horseman.

Ryland English: from the land of the reeds.

S

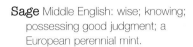

Sage Middle English: wise; knowing; possessing good judgment; a European perennial mint.

Salvatore Latin: of the Savior. **Sal**, **Sally**.

Sam Hebrew: to hear.

Samson Hebrew: sun-like; magnificent; robust.

Samuel Old English: from the sandy brook. Samuel L. Jackson, American actor. **Sam, Sammy, Samson**.

Sanborn English: from the sandy brook.

Sanders Greek: one who helps humanity; son of Alexander. **Sandor, Saunders**.

Sandor a form of Sanders. **Sander**.

Sandy a form of Sanford and Alexander.

Sanford Anglo-Saxon: one who lives near a sandy stream. **Sandy**.

Sascha a form of Alexander. **Sasha**.

Satchel Middle English: a rucksack or small carrier. Satchel Paige, American baseball player.

Saul Hebrew: asked for; hoped for. Saul Bellow, Canadian-born writer.

Saunders a form of Sanders.

Sawyer Celtic: one who cuts wood.

Scott Latin: one from Scotland; one who is tattooed. F. Scott Fitzgerald, American writer. **Scotty**, **Scottie**.

Seamus a form of James.

Sean a form of John.

Seaton English: from the settlement by the sea.

Sebastian Greek: majestic; venerated; lovely. **Sebastien**, **Sebastiano**, **Bastien**.

Selby Teutonic: farm by the manor.

Selwyn Teutonic: friend of the manor; wooded area; feral.

Sennett French: elderly one.

Sergeant Middle English: one who helps; assistant.

Serge Latin: one who serves. **Sergei**, **Sergio**.

Sergei Russian: a form of Serge.

Sergio Italian: a form of Serge. Sergio Leone, Italian spaghetti western film director.

Seth Hebrew: chosen; appointed.

Seton Anglo-Saxon: from the seaside.

Seymour Old French: from St. Maur; also, Teutonic: from the wild seacoast.

Shandy Old English: boisterous; out of control.

Shane a form of John.

Shaw Anglo-Saxon: one who lives in the grove.

Shea Irish: learned; majestic; from the village of the shea trees.

Sheehan Irish: diminutive; serene.

Sheffield Old English: one who is from the jagged field. **Fields**.

Shelby English: from the village of the willow trees.

Sheldon Anglo-Saxon: one who is from the ridge. **Shelly**.

Shepard Anglo-Saxon: one who watches sheep. **Shep**.

Sheridan Celtic: in the natural habitat; uncultivated.

Sherman Anglo-Saxon: one who shaves sheep; one who cuts cloth.

Sherwin Anglo-Saxon: faithful friend.

Sherwood Anglo-Saxon: illuminated woodlands.

Sidney Old French: from St. Denis.

Sidney Lumet, American film director. **Sid**.

Sigmund Teutonic: victorious protector. Sigmund Freud, Moravian-born founder of psychoanalysis. **Ziggy**.

Silas Latin: person from the forest; deity of the woods. Silas Marner, protagonist of a George Eliot novel of the same name. **Si**.

Simm a form of Simon.

Simon Hebrew: one who hears; dutiful. **Simm**.

Sinclair Latin: virtuous; memorable light. Sinclair Lewis, American writer.

Skip Old Norse: captain of a boat. **Skipper**, **Skippy**.

Skyler Dutch: schoolmaster; scholar. **Sky**, **Skye**, **Skylar**, **Schuyler**.

Sloan Celtic: a soldier.

Smith Old English: blacksmith. **Smyth**.

Solomon Hebrew: peaceful man; judicious.

Somerset Old English: one who is from the place of summer.

Sonny North American: young boy. Sonny Corleone, fictional mobster of Mario Puzo's *The Godfather*.

Spencer Middle English: one who supplies necessities.

Spike English: uncontrollable clump of hair.

Stacy Greek: one to be restored to life; also, Latin: consistent; rich.

Stafford Anglo-Saxon: one who is from the place near the river crossing.

Standish Old English: stony orchard.

Stanford Old English: rocky river crossing. Stanford Blatch, fictional character on *Sex and the City*. **Stannie**.

Stanhope Old English: rock-strewn gorge.

Stanley Anglo-Saxon: stony ground. **Stan**, **Stannie**.

Stanton Anglo-Saxon: one who is from a rocky location.

Stedman Anglo-Saxon: one who possesses a farm.

Stephan a form of Steven. **Stéphane**.

Stephen a form of Steven.

Sterling Teutonic: actually having much value; genuine.

Steven Greek: coronet; wreath. Steven Spielberg, American filmmaker. **Steve**, **Stevie**, **Stephen**, **Stephan**, **Stefan**, **Stéphane** **Étienne**, **Esteban**.

Stewart Anglo-Saxon: one who runs the manor. **Stuart**.

Stillman Anglo-Saxon: calm; good; diplomatic.

Stilton English: a cheese with blue veins made from cows' milk and cream.

Stoddard Old English: one who cares for horses.

Stone Middle English: earthen rock or hardened mineral. Stone Phillips, American news reporter.

Storm English: a tempest or squall. Storm Field, American meteorologist.

Stuart a form of Stewart.

Styles Old English: of the steps.

Sumner Latin: one who calls out.

Sutton Anglo-Saxon: one who is from a southern place.

Sweeney Irish: a little hero.

Sylvester English and German: one who is from the forest.

Tab Old German: one who drums. Tab Hunter, American actor.

Taddeus Hebrew: full of acclaim; courageous. **Tad, Taddie, Thaddeus, Thad.**

Talbot Old French: illuminated as the vale; bloodhound. **Talbert.**

Talcott Old English: from the lakeside. **Talcot.**

Talen English French: a claw. **Talon.**

Tanner Old English: one who works with leather.

Tate Teutonic: full of mirth. Tate Donovan, American actor.

Tavis Irish: twin. **Tavish.**

Tayce a form of Tracy.

Taylor Latin: tailor; one who modifies.

Ted a form of Edward. **Teddy.**

Telford Old English: from the shallow river crossing; also, French: an armor cutter and fitter.

Templeton Old English: holy city.

Tennessee Native American: a state. Tennessee Williams, American playwright.

Terrence Latin: gentle; soft. **Terry**, **Thierry**.

Terry a form of Terrence.

Thaddeus a form of Taddeus. **Thad**, **Thaddie**.

Thane Anglo-Saxon: one who follows the king; soldier.

Thatcher Anglo-Saxon: a roof thatcher.

Thayer Teutonic: one who belongs to the army.

Theo a form of Theodore.

Theodore Greek: bequest of God. Theodore Roosevelt, 26th American president. **Theo**, **Ted**, **Teddy**.

Theron Greek: a huntsman.

Thibault Teutonic: most courageous prince of the people.

Thierry a form of Terrence.

Thomas Hebrew: a twin. Thomas Edison, American inventor. **Tom**, **Tommy**.

Thorndike Old English: one who is from the thorny shore. **Thorny**.

Thornton Anglo-Saxon: one who is from a village of thorns. **Thorny**.

Thorpe Anglo-Saxon: one who is from the little town.

Thurman Scandinavian: guarded by Thor. Thurman Munson, American baseball player.

Thurston Scandinavian: Thor's prized stone.

Tibor Hungarian: from the River Tiber. Tibor Kalman, Hungarian-born graphic designer.

Tierney Irish: monarch.

Tiger Middle English: formidable, audacious, or assertive. Tiger Woods, American golfer.

Tilden Anglo-Saxon: one who is from the affluent vale.

Tilford Old English: one who is from the fruitful stream.

Timothy Greek: one who worships a deity. Tip O'Neill, American politician. **Tim**, **Timmy**, **Tip**.

Tito a form of Titus.

Titus Greek: large being. **Tito**.

Tobias Hebrew: God is good. **Toby**, **Tobie**.

Toby a form of Tobias. **Tobie**.

Todd Latin: a fox.

Toland Anglo-Saxon: from soil that has a tariff.

Tony a form of Anthony.

Topher a form of Christopher. Topher Grace, American actor. **Tiffer**.

Tinsley Old English: from the fortified field.

Townsend Anglo-Saxon: one who is from the end of town.

Tracy Latin: courageous soldier. Spencer Tracy, American actor. **Trace**, **Tayce**.

Travers Latin: one who is from the fork in the road. **Travis**.

Travis a form of Travers.

Tremayne Celtic: from the land near the stone circle. **Tremaine**.

Trent Latin: fast-flowing brook.

Trevor Celtic: sagacious; thoughtful; careful; wise man.

Trey Middle English: three; die, card, or domino with the number three.

Trilby British: soft felt hat with an indented crown; from the novel *Trilby* by George du Maurier.

Trinity Latin: three; name taken in honor of the Christian Holy Trinity.

Tristan Celtic: the name of a protagonist of a tragic medieval romance, between Tristram and Isolde. **Tristram**.

Troy Old French: one who has curly hair. Troy Donohue, American actor.

True Middle English: steadfast; loyal.

Truman Anglo-Saxon: loyal person.

Tucker Old English: one who tucks or folds cloth.

Tully Latin: devout; calm.

Turner Old French: tournament winner.

Tyler Anglo-Saxon: one who fashions bricks or tiles.

Tynan Irish: dark one. **Ty**.

Tyrone Greek: leader with total authority. Tyrone Power, American actor. **Ty**.

Tyson Old French: one who incites. **Tyrell**.

Ulysses Greek: livid; one who hates deceitfulness and unfairness. From Homer's *The Odyssey*. Ulysses S. Grant, 18th American president.

Umberto Italian: intense, celebrated soldier.

Upton Anglo-Saxon: one who comes from the village on the hill. Upton Sinclair, American writer.

Urban Latin: city dweller; urbane; gracious.

Uriah Hebrew: God is luminescent. **Uri**.

Van Dutch: son of. Van Johnson, American actor.

Vance Dutch: one who harvests; Van's son.

Vaughn Celtic: small. Vaughn Meader, American satirist. **Vaughan**.

Vernon Latin: young; new; alive. **Vern**.

Victor Latin: triumphant. **Vic**.

Vidal Spanish: life.

Vincent Latin: vanquisher. Vincent Price, American actor. **Vince, Vinnie, Vin, Vicente**.

Virgil Latin: one who bears a rod or staff; alive; potent.

Vito Latin: vital; thriving.

Vladimir Slavic: one who is of noble renown; prince of everything and everyone. **Vlad, Wladimir**.

W

Wade Anglo-Saxon: one who resides the crossing in the river; nomad.

Wadsworth Anglo-Saxon: one who is from Wade's land.

Wainwright Old English: one who fashions wagons.

Waite Middle English: one who guards the security of others; defender.

Wakefield Old English: damp meadow.

Walcott Anglo-Saxon: bungalow with walls.

Walden Teutonic: potent sovereign; one who is from the woods.

Waldo Teutonic: commanding; leader.

Walford Old English: from the Welshman's stream.

Walker Anglo-Saxon: one who walks in the woods. Walker Evans, American photographer.

Wallace Anglo-Saxon: one who is from Wales; outsider; unknown person. Wallace Shawn, American playwright and actor. **Wally, Walsh.**

Walsh a form of Wallace.

Walter Teutonic: strong soldier; head of state. Protagonist of James Thurber's *The Secret Life of Walter Mitty*. **Wally**, **Gautier**.

Walton Old English: a village with a wall surrounding it; one who is from a village in the woods.

Ward Teutonic: one who guards the security of others.

Waring Latin: honest; careful; defense.

Warner Teutonic: a soldier who is the last line of protection.

Warren Teutonic: a defender; one who guards wild animals.

Warrick a form of Warwick.

Warwick Teutonic: bastion; solid, defending leader. **Warrick**.

Washburn Old English: one is from the floodplain of a rivulet.

Washington Anglo-Saxon: one who comes from the home of a wise, astute person.

Watson Anglo-Saxon: Walter's son.

Waverly Old English: one who is from a meadow of fluttering aspens.

Waylon Teutonic: the ground by the path. Waylon Jennings, American country singer.

Wayne Teutonic: one who fashions wagons.

Webb Old English: a weaver.

Webster Anglo-Saxon: one who weaves textiles. Noah Webster, American lexicographer.

Welby Scandinavian: one who comes from the ranch near the spring.

Weldon Teutonic: one who is from the natural spring on the knoll.

Welford Old English: one who comes from the well by the stream.

Wells Old English: one who is from the natural spring.

Wendell Teutonic: one who journeys. Oliver Wendell Holmes, American jurist, author, and physician.

Werner German, Dutch, and Scandinavian: an army soldier. Werner Klemperer, German-born actor.

Wesley Anglo-Saxon: a western plain. John Wesley, 18th-century British religious leader. **Wes.**

Westcott Teutonic: one who lives in the cabin in the west.

Weston Old English: one who is from a village in the west. **West.**

Whitby Scandinavian: near the white town. **Whit.**

Whitney Anglo-Saxon: a white island.

Wilbur Teutonic: strong-willed; illuminated; intelligent.

Wilfred Teutonic: resolute peacemaker.

Willard Teutonic: strong; brave.

Willem a form of William. Willem Dafoe, American actor.

William Teutonic: strong armor; the helmet. **Bill, Billy, Will, Willie, Willy, Liam, Willis, Wills, Willem, Wolf, Wolfie, Guilliame.**

Willis a form of William.

Wilson Teutonic: William's son.

Wilton Old English: from the village well.

Win a form of Windsor.

Windsor Teutonic: near a crook in the waterway; border created by a river. **Win.**

Winfield Anglo-Saxon: one who is from a friend's meadow.

Winkle British: to get something or extract with effort. **Winkie, Wink.**

Winslow Teutonic: one who is from a friend's hill. **Win.**

Winston Anglo-Saxon: welcoming village. Sir Winston Churchill, British prime minister.

Winter Middle English: season between fall and spring; the colder part of the year.

Winthrop Teutonic: one who is from a friend's town. **Winthorp.**

Wolcott Old English: a wolf's cabin.

Wolf a form of William and Wolfgang. **Wolfie.**

Wolfgang Old German: a wolf that is moving forward. Wolfgang Amadeus Mozart, 18th-century Austrian composer. **Wolf, Wolfie.**

Woodrow Anglo-Saxon: one who is from a forest path; hedge close to a wooded area. Woodrow Wilson, 28th American president. **Woody.**

Woodward Anglo-Saxon: guardian of the woods.

Worth Old English: one who is from a farm.

Wright Anglo-Saxon: artist who works with wood; carpenter.

Wyatt Old French: little soldier; escort. Wyatt Earp, American western lawman.

Wylie Anglo-Saxon: charismatic; jolly. **Wiley.**

Wynn Old Welsh: one who is cheerful and fair.

Xander a form of Alexander.

Xavier Arabic: bright; magnificent. St. Francis Xavier, 16th-century patron saint.

Yahoo North American: variation of "yo ho", an interjection used to attract attention. Yahoo Serious, Australian actor and filmmaker.

Yale Teutonic: donor; also, Old English: corner of the earth.

Yancy Native American: person from England; Yankee.

Yates Anglo-Saxon: gateway.

Yonah a form of Jonah.

York Latin: hallowed tree.

Yossi Hebrew: a form of Joseph.

Young Middle English: recently come into being; new.

Yves Scandinavian: one who uses a bow.

Zachariah a form of Zachary.

Zacharias a form of Zachary.

Zachary Hebrew: considered by God. Zachary Taylor, 12th American president. **Zach, Zack, Zachariah, Zacharias.**

Zander a form of Alexander.

Zane a form of John.

Zeb Hebrew: gift of God.

Zebulon Hebrew: to honor; to praise. Zebulon Pike, 19th-century American explorer.

Zeke a form of Ezekiel.

Zev Hebrew: wolf.

Fashionable Names Through the Decades

Here are the most popular names in America, through the years. It's fun to look back and see how many names have made a comeback, and how many others probably never will.

1880

Girls

Mary
Annie
Elizabeth
Margaret
Minnie
Emma
Martha
Alice
Marie
Sarah

Boys

John
William
Charles
George
James
Joseph
Frank
Henry
Thomas
Harry

1900

Girls

Mary
Helen
Anna
Margaret
Ruth
Elizabeth
Marie
Rose
Florence
Bertha

Boys

John
William
James
George
Charles
Joseph
Frank
Henry
Robert
Harry

1920

Girls

Mary
Dorothy
Helen
Margaret
Ruth
Virginia
Elizabeth
Anna
Mildred
Betty

Boys

John
William
James
Robert
Joseph
Charles
George
Edward
Thomas
Frank

1940

Girls

Mary
Barbara
Patricia
Carol
Judith
Betty
Nancy
Maria
Margaret
Linda

Boys

James
Robert
John
William
Richard
Charles
David
Thomas
Donald
Ronald

1960

Girls

Mary
Susan
Maria
Karen
Lisa
Linda
Donna
Patricia
Debra
Deborah

Boys

David
Michael
John
James
Robert
Mark
William
Richard
Thomas
Steven

1980

Girls

Jennifer
Jessica
Amanda
Melissa
Sarah
Nicole
Heather
Amy
Michelle
Elizabeth

Boys

Michael
Jason
Christopher
David
James
Matthew
John
Joshua
Robert
Daniel

2000

Girls

Emily
Hannah
Madison
Ashley
Sarah
Alexis
Samantha
Jessica
Taylor
Elizabeth

Boys

Jacob
Michael
Matthew
Joshua
Christopher
Nicholas
Andrew
Joseph
Daniel
Tyler

Girls' and Boys' Names from Around the World

Here are some popular names from all over the globe. Some translate beautifully; others create that little extra twist that make an over-used name fresh and modern.

African

Girls

Anana
Faizah
Halima
Jendyi
Keisha
Lateefah
Nailah
Raziya
Salihah
Takiyah

Boys

Chike
Dakarai
Faraji
Gamba
Jayvyn
Keon
Mansa
Naeem
Razi
Tabari

Arabic

Girls

Aiesha
Bibi
Cala
Farah
Kadira
Malika
Peridot
Rana
Wasima
Zaza

Boys

Ahmed
Emir
Faisal
Hakim
Imam
Jamal
Kalil
Mohammed
Walid
Zia

British

Chinese

Girls

Afton
Bedelia
Clover
Darby
Edwina
Merivale
Nellwyn
Petula
Rowena
Whitney

Girls

An
Bo
Chyou
Genji
Hua
Jin
Lian
Mingmei
Sun
Tao

Boys

Ainsley
Cedric
Delwyn
Fenwick
Litton
Northrop
Oakes
Penley
Stanwick
Wesley

Boys

Bo
Chen
Ho
Li
Manchu
Ming
Shen
Sun
Wen
Yuan

Dutch

French

Girls

Brandy
Dorothea
Kaatje
Karel
Lena
Maieka
Nelleke
Saskia
Schylar
Tyrne

Girls

Aimée
Bari
Cérise
Chantal
Emme
Fleur
Ghislaine
Marielle
Megane
Yvette

Boys

Arne
Claus
Dirk
Hugo
Joost
Karel
Maarten
Piet
Rutger
Wim

Boys

Didier
Étienne
Gaston
Henri
Jacques
Luc
Pierre
Remy
Thibaud
Yves

German

Girls
Adelaide
Bluma
Frederika
Greta
Katrine
Liesl
Mathilda
Nixie
Rosamond
Steffi

Boys
Dieter
Gottfried
Heinrich
Johannes
Josef
Karl
Ludwig
Reinhold
Stefan
Wim

Greek

Girls
Aphrodite
Beryl
Calliope
Daphne
Eleni
Ianthe
Lydia
Melanie
Ophelia
Theodora

Boys
Achilles
Christos
Darius
Erasmus
Hercules
Jason
Lucas
Nestor
Panos
Stavros

Hawaiian

Girls

Aloha
Haleigha
Iolana
Kalea
Keilana
Leilani
Makani
Mily
Noelani
Wanika

Boys

Bane
Havika
Kahoku
Kai
Kalani
Kale
Keona
Makani
Meka
Palani

Hebrew

Girls

Aliya
Chaya
Etana
Galia
Kezia
Malka
Rahel
Shifra
Tamar
Yael

Boys

Barak
Chaim
Dov
Eleazar
Gideon
Isaac
Levi
Mayer
Noam
Ronit

Irish

Girls
Ashling
Brynna
Clodagh
Darby
Eilish
Erin
Fenella
Fiona
Maeve
Siobhan

Boys
Aidan
Brody
Dermot
Eamon
Finbar
Kieran
Liam
Padraig
Roan
Tiernan

Italian

Girls
Alessandra
Cara
Fiorenza
Giovanna
Isabella
Luciana
Marietta
Paola
Romana
Vittoria

Boys
Carlo
Enrico
Giuseppe
Lorenzo
Marcello
Nuncio
Paolo
Stephano
Umberto
Vittore

Japanese

Girls
Aiko
Fujita
Gin
Haruko
Keiko
Miyoko
Nori
Reiko
Takako
Yumi

Boys
Akira
Botan
Dai
Hiroshi
Kiyoshi
Mamoru
Ryozo
Shuichi
Tomi
Yasuo

Jewish

Girls
Enya
Freyde
Fruma
Hadassah
Hinda
Leba
Maida
Mindel
Shayndel
Syshe

Boys
Binyamin
Hershel
Hesh
Mandel
Moishe
Selig
Shlomo
Volf
Yehuda
Zelig

Latin

Girls

Cadence
Delphine
Felicity
Honora
Isola
Jocelyn
Perdita
Sabina
Trista
Verbena

Boys

Adrian
Felix
Horatio
Inigo
Marcus
Nigel
Prosper
Rex
Tarquin
Victor

Native American

Girls

Aponi
Bly
Chenoa
Fala
Kiona
Minda
Onida
Shysie
Taima
Waneta

Boys

Cheyenne
Dakota
Elyu
Jacie
Lakota
Namide
Pilan
Sakima
Tyee
Yancy

Russian

Girls

Anastasia
Ekaterina
Feodora
Galina
Oksana
Raisa
Sonya
Talia
Vanya
Yelena

Boys

Boris
Fjodor
Ilya
Dostya
Lev
Mikhail
Oleg
Pavel
Vasily
Yuri

Scandinavian

Girls

Anneliese
Birgitta
Erika
Katrine
Mia
Nissa
Ola
Thorborg
Ulrike
Vanja

Boys

Anders
Frans
Josef
Karl
Lars
Olaf
Per
Thorvald
Verner
Waldemar

Spanish

Girls
Carmelita
Engracia
Hermelinda
Jacinta
Maribel
Pilar
Rosario
Soledad
Tia
Vittoria

Boys
Alejandro
Carlos
Diego
Enrique
Federico
Javier
Luis
Miguel
Pablo
Renald

Multiple Names

When you're planning for twins, triplets, or more, choosing
names can be complicated. The names need to blend
beautifully, but be unique—just like your babies. Here are
some fun combinations that work.

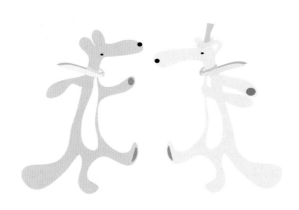

Great Combos

a

Abbie and Ned
Adam and Bailey
Addison and Alistair
Adeline and Morgan
Ainsley, Kirsten, and Miranda
Alejandro and Javier
Alex, Zach, and Bart
Amberose and Ashlyn
Andrew and Charles
Angela, Teresa, and Caterina
Armand and Regis
Aubrey and Sherman

b

Beau, Finn, and Grant
Ben and Noah
Bennett and William
Bradley and Maxwell
Brooke, Gabrielle, and Ainsley

c

Caleb and Ethan
Candace and Aimee
Carleton and Avery
Carlie, Syndey, and Michaela
Caroline and Stephanie
Carrie and Carly
Carter and Cooper
Carter and Hazel
Casey and Daniel
Catherine, Claire, and Caroline
Charlotte and Catherine
Chloe, Caitlin, and Courtney
Colette, Chloe, and Charlotte
Crispin, Oliver, and George

d

Daffodil and Jocelyn
Daisy and Fiona
Dalton and Fisher
Daniel and Merielle
Daphne and Laurel
David and Tracey
Declan and Avril
Desmond and Duncan
Dulcie and Caitlyn

e

Edward and Alexander
Eilish and Kate
Elena, Isabel, and Pilar
Elijah and Fanny
Ellie, Sophie, and Porter
Elspeth and Ambrose
Esmé and Zoë
Everett and Harper

f

Farleigh and Jacob
Felicity and Imogen
Fergus and Angus
Fletcher and Aidan
Forrest and Arden
Francesca and Giorgio

g

Gabriel and Weston
Gabrielle and Veronica
Gareth and Jasper
Geoffrey and George
Giselle and Gabriella
Grace and Esmé
Grant and Hayden
Gregory and Harrison

h

Hamilton and Harrison
Harper and Hazel
Harrison and Parker
Harry and Rosie
Hazel and Ruby
Hollis, Ava, and Hunter
Honey and Darcy
Hortense and Daffodil
Hugo, Jasper, and Harvey
Hyacinth and Harry

i

India and Esmé
Iris, Rose, and Lily
Isabel and Fiona
Isaiah and Jeremy

j

Jacob and Hunter
James and Bartholomew
Jameson and Jackson
Jessamyn and Sebastian
Jesse and Jody
Jessica and Violet
Joshua and Zev

k

Katie and Megan
Kaylin and Ashley
Keeley and Tyler
Kelly and Kyle
Kendra and Grace
Kira, Kelsey, and Katelyn

l

Lachlan and Jonah
Lark and Kendra
Laurel and Daphne
Lavender and Abbie
Levi and Daniel
Liam and Michael
Lily, Daisy, and James
Lisbeth and Charlotte
Lissie and Alastair
Lucie and Yardley
Lucy and Lavender

m

Mabel and Joe
Mackenzie, Olivia, and Rachel
Malcolm, Gregory, and Michael
Maraid and James
Marissa and Juliana
Mark and Violet
Mary Jane and Jackson
Maude, Primrose, Lucy,
    and Tess
Max and Katie
Maxwell, Lucas, and Jackson
Megan and Pansy
Melinda and Xavier
Melissa and Declan
Mereille and Marilee
Michael and Michaela
Michah and Asher
Miranda and Phoebe
Milo and Jane
Morgan and Zoë
Moses and Taylor

n

Nancy and Elizabeth
Nathan and Wiley
Neil and Tess
Nia and Laurel

O

Olive and Norris
Oliver and Malcolm
Olivia, Gemma, and Isabel
Owen and Parker

p

Paige, Aubrey, and Lindsey
Pamela and Patricia
Parker and Pansy
Patience and Lilac
Penelope and Julianne
Pepper and Steven
Peter and Thomas
Philip, Peter, and Henry
Phipps and Kate
Phoebe and Daphne
Pippa and Keely
Pixie and Lucy
Plum and Poppy
Porter and Carter
Posy and Prudence
Preston and Kyle
Primrose and Posy

q

Quinnie and Jenice

r

Rebecca and Jessica
Regan and Vincent
Reyanne and Robert
Riley and Alison
Robert and Richard
Rory and Windsor
Rosie, Daisy, and Rebecca
Ruby and Abigail
Rupert, Peregrine, and
   Quentin
Ryan and Ross

s

Sarah, Rowan, and Katherine
Sebastian, Duncan, and
   Ambrose
Serena and Phoebe
Sheldon and Louise
Sherman and Seymour
Sophie and Charles
Stella and Grace
Stephen and Eamon
Stuart and Tucker

t

Tabitha and Tess
Tessa and Willow
Thea and Addison
Tinka and Jed
Tobias and Elijah
Trevor and Steven
Tucker and Sabrina
Tyler and Liam

V

Valerie and Vanessa
Vincenzo and Guiseppe
Violet and Ruby

W

Walker and Tamsin
Weston and Gideon
Whitney and Taylor
William and Walker
Willoughby and Lucas

y

Yves and Zoë

Z

Zachary and Michael

Bad Combos

a

Alexander, Zachariah,
and Bart
Andressa and Vanessa
Andrew and Andrea
April, May, and June
Archie and Veronica

b

Bart and Lisa
Becky and Tom
Bill and Hillary
Brooke and Lynn

c

Caden, Corbin, and Colin
Caleb, Parker, and Tanner
Cara and Mia
Carrie and Candy
Carleen and Carlyn
Cassius and Calliope
Charlotte, Chloe, and Colette
Cole, Chandler, and Conner

d

Doris and Rock

e

Ed and Ward
Elizabeth and Isabel
(Lizzy and Izzy)
Emerson and Ethan

f

Fred and Ethel
Fred and Ginger
Fred and Wilma

g

Genevieve, Gwendolyn, and
    Guinevere (where's
    Gwyneth?)
George and Georgina
Gertie and Trudy

h

Haley and Holly
Hamlet and Ophelia
Hansel and Gretel
Harold and Maude
Holly and Dolly
Homer and Marge

i

Ike and Mike

j

Jack and Jackie
Jack and Jill
James and Bartholomew
Jared, Joshua, and Jacob
John and Yoko
John, David, and Gavin
Joseph and Josephine
June and Ward

k

Kenzie, Kylee, and Katie
Kyle, Kellen, and Kieran

l

Lauren and Humphrey
Liz and Richard
Lois and Clark
London, Logan, and Landis
Lucy and Desi
Lucy and Ethel
Lucy and Ricky
Lydia, Sophia, and Maria

m

Madison, Magdalen, and
  Madeline
Madison, Marissa, and Merilee
  (Maddy, Marrie, and Merrie)
Mickey and Minnie

n

Nathan, Morgan, and Julian
Nicholas and Alexandra
Nick and Nora
Noreen and Doreen

o

Owen, Duncan, Ivan, Evan,
  and Ian

p

Peter and Wendy
Peyton, Paige, and Presley

r

Romulus and Remus
Ronnie and Nancy
Rory, Tori, Corey, and Laurie

s

Sage and Ginger
Sebastian, Jackson, and
  Maxim
Shanna, Shayna, and Shawna
Summer and August

t

Tarzan and Jane
Tianna, Brianna, and Johanna
Tipper and Al
Tristan and Isolde

w

William, Samuel, and David
Woody and Mia
Woody and Soon Yi

z

Zander and Alexander
Zane, Zander, Zaire, and Zion

Fun Names

Here are some delightful little lists of delicious little names.

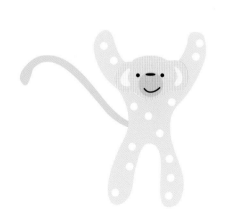

Angel Girls

Angela	Faith	Heaven	Prudence
Bliss	Felicity	Honor	Seraphina
Charity	Grace	Hope	True
Destiny	Harmony	Patience	
Ever	Haven		

Colorful Girls

Blanca	Ione	Rose	Violet
Blue	Lavender	Ruby	
Gray	Lilac	Sapphire	
Iole	Red	Silver	

Flower Girls

Angelica	Flora	Laurel	Poppy
Camilla	Heather	Lilac	Posy
Clover	Holly	Lilly	Rose
Daffodil	Hyacinth	Marigold	Saffron
Daisy	Iris	Pansy	Tansy
Fern	Ivy	Peony	Violet
Fleur	Jasmine	Petunia	Zinnia

Cuter Than Cute Girls

Amber	Ivy	Poppy	Sweetie
Baby	Jade	Rose	Vicky
Daisy	Jasmine	Ruby	Willow
Fifi	Maggie	Sage	
Honey	Minnie	Sugar	
Iris	Peaches	Summer	

Grandma Girls

Ada	Doris	Irma	Roberta
Agatha	Dorothy	Jean	Selma
Agnes	Edwina	Laverne	Shirley
Arlene	Eleanore	Lillian	Sylvia
Barbara	Enid	Lucille	Thelma
Bernice	Estelle	Marjorie	Ursula
Bertha	Ethel	Mildred	Wanda
Betty	Eunice	Myra	Zelda
Beulah	Gladys	Myrtle	
Dolores	Gloria	Norma	
Dorcas	Hilda	Rhoda	

Gem Girls

Amber	Coral	Goldie	Opal
Amethyst	Crystal	Ivory	Pearl
Beryl	Emerald	Jade	Ruby
Bijou	Garnet	Jasper	Sapphire
Cameo	Gemma	Jewel	

Perfect Girls

Abigail	Emma	Kimberly	Rachel
Alexa	Esmé	Laura	Rebecca
Alexandra	Gabrielle	Lauren	Riley
Alison	Grace	Lindsey	Rose
Amanda	Hailey	Lisa	Sophia
Anabel	Hannah	Lucy	Stephanie
Ashley	Isabel	Madison	Taylor
Avery	Jade	Margaret	Victoria
Brooke	Jane	Mary	Virginia
Caroline	Jasmine	Megan	Zoë
Charlotte	Jessica	Melissa	
Chloe	Julia	Mia	
Danielle	Kaitlyn	Nicole	
Elizabeth	Kaylin	Olivia	
Emily	Kendall	Paige	

Girly Girls

Alice	Grace	Maisie	Violet
Amelia	Honor	Rosie	Zoë
Anna	Josie	Ruby	
Daisy	Lily	Sadie	
Dixie	Lucy	Tess	

Sweet Girls

Adri	Cecilia	Kaitlyn	Merry
Alexandra	Chérie	Kelsey	Missy
Alicia	Emma	Lacey	Scarlet
Annabel	Emmeline	Laurel	Serena
Anastasia	Heather	Lauren	Shelby
Angelica	Jasmine	Lilac	Trish
Angelina	Jenica	Liliana	
Arabella	Jessica	Megan	
Ariana	Juliana	Melissa	

Pretty Girls

Amelie	Chiara	Danica	Rosie
Arabella	Clea	Esmé	Tessa
Chantal	Daisy	Lily	Thea

Middle Names for Girls

Anne	Grace	Lark	Rose
Beth	Jade	Maeve	Sloan
Blair	James	Maude	Spencer
Brooke	Jane	Morgan	Tessa
Carter	Kate	Nell	Winnie

Handsome and Smart Boys

Aidan	Ethan	Jonathan	Philip
Alexander	Evan	Joseph	Richard
Andrew	Harrison	Joshua	Riley
Anthony	Harry	Kevin	Robert
Benjamin	Henry	Kyle	Ryan
Brandon	Hunter	Lucas	Steven
Caleb	Jack	Matthew	Thomas
Carter	Jackson	Michael	Trevor
Charles	Jaden	Nathan	Tyler
Daniel	James	Nicholas	William
David	Jameson	Paul	Zachary
Dylan	Jason	Peter	
Edward	John		

Middle Names for Boys

Benjamin	Frederick	Joshua	Parker
Carter	George	Max	Spencer
Daniel	James	Michael	Steven
Edward	Jay	Morgan	William

Old Man Boys

Alvin	Earl	Hiram	Sidney
Archibald	Elmer	Howard	Stanley
Arnold	Elmo	Hubert	Vernon
Barney	Ernest	Irving	Victor
Burton	Eugene	Irwin	Waldo
Donald	Herbert	Leonard	Wendell
Dwayne	Herman	Melvin	Wilfred

Biblical Girls

Esther	Rachel	Salome	Tamar
Hannah	Rebecca	Sarah	

Biblical Boys

Aaron	Ezekiel	Joshua	Raphael
Benjamin	Ezra	Isaiah	Samuel
Caleb	Gabriel	Jacob	
Eli	Gideon	Levi	
Elijah	Isaac	Noah	

Great Unisex Names

Blair	Dakota	Jamie	Regan
Brady	Dana	Jordan	Robin
Cameron	Darby	Kendall	Shelby
Campbell	Devon	Kyle	Sloane
Carlton	Bailey	Madison	Taylor
Carson	Harper	Morgan	Walker
Carter	Hunter	Murphy	

Royal Girls

Alexandra	Diana	Margaret	Sarah
Alice	Eleanor	Martha	Sophia
Anne	Elizabeth	Mary	Victoria
Beatrice	Eugenie	Matilda	Zara
Caroline	Gabriella	Maud	
Catherine	Isabel	Philippa	
Charlotte	Jane	Rose	

Royal Boys

Albert	Duncan	James	Peter
Alfred	Edward	John	Philip
Andrew	Frederick	Louis	Richard
Arthur	George	Michael	Stephen
Charles	Harry	Nicholas	William
David	Henry	Paul	

243

Nicknames for Girls and Boys

Remember, that tiny little baby will one day be an adult. Give that child a great, grown-up name. Then, you can consider one of these cuter-than-cute nicknames.

Nicknames for Girls

Babs
Baby
Bambi
Bebe
Bess
Betta
Bibi
Binnie
Birdie
Bitsy
Bobbie
Booboo
Brandi
Bubbles
Bunny
Cammie
Candy
Cassie
Coco
Cricket
Cuddles
Daisy
Darly
Debbie

Debs
Dixie
Dodie
Dolly
Dory
Dottie
Drea
Emmie
Estee
Fifi
Florrie
Flossie
Frankie
Frannie
Freddie
Gertie
Glennie
Gwen
Gwynnie
Hattie
Kat
Kitty
Lettie
Libby

Lissa
Livvy
Lottie
Lovie
Lulu
Maggie
Mamie
Martie
Maudie
Maxie
Megs
Millie
Mimi
Minnie
Missy
Misty
Muffy
Nan
Nanny
Nellie
Nessa
Nessie
Noni
Peaches

Pebbles
Pepper
Pippa
Polly
Poodle
Poopoo
Puppy
Sadie
Sissy
Sister
Stella
Sweetie
Tibbie
Tillie
Tinky
Tish
Tori
Trish
Trudy
Winnie
Zannie

Nicknames for Boys

Angel	Butch	Gibby	Ray
Benno	Chaz	Gram	Robin
Berdie	Chip	Jock	Stinky
Biff	Chuck	Joe	Tad
Billie	Dix	Joey	Taddie
Bobby	Duckie	King	Teddo
Bobbo	Duffy	Lucky	Tibby
Bobs	Duke	Ned	Tippy
Bram	Dunn	Neddie	Tottie
Bubba	Dusty	Petey	Trey
Buck	Fatty	Piggy	Wills
Bud	Fee	Pip	Zander
Buddy	Feeney	Pooh	
Busby	Fofo	Prince	
Buster	Frankie	Rafe	

Name Worksheets

Here is some space to scribble down any names that tickle your fancy. Years from now, you'll laugh and laugh that you even considered those names.

It's a Girl

We Love These Names . . . .
. . . .
. . . .
. . . .
. . . .
. . . .
. . . .
. . . .

Everyone Loves These Names . . . .
. . . .
. . . .
. . . .

The Best Loved Baby Names . . . .
. . . .
. . . .
. . . .

It's a Boy

We Love These Names . . . .

. . . .

. . . .

. . . .

. . . .

. . . .

. . . .

. . . .

Everyone Loves These Names . . . .

. . . .

. . . .

. . . .

The Best Loved Baby Names . . . .

. . . .

. . . .

. . . .

It's a Girl

We Love These Names . . . .
. . . .
. . . .
. . . .
. . . .
. . . .
. . . .

Everyone Loves These Names . . . .
. . . .
. . . .
. . . .

The Best Loved Baby Names . . . .
. . . .
. . . .
. . . .

It's a Boy

We Love These Names . . . .

. . . .

. . . .

. . . .

. . . .

. . . .

. . . .

. . . .

Everyone Loves These Names. . . . .

. . . .

. . . .

. . . .

The Best Loved Baby Names. . . . .

. . . .

. . . .

. . . .

It's a Girl

We Love These Names . . . .
. . . .
. . . .
. . . .
. . . .
. . . .
. . . .
. . . .

Everyone Loves These Names . . . .
. . . .
. . . .
. . . .

The Best Loved Baby Names . . . .
. . . .
. . . .
. . . .

It's a Boy

We Love These Names . . . .
. . . .
. . . .
. . . .
. . . .
. . . .
. . . .
. . . .

Everyone Loves These Names . . . .
. . . .
. . . .
. . . .

The Best Loved Baby Names . . . .
. . . . , ...
. . . .
. . . .

Notes